50 Korean-Texan BBQ Recipes for Home

By: Kelly Johnson

Table of Contents

- Korean Beef Short Ribs (Galbi)
- Spicy Pork Belly (Samgyeopsal)
- Korean BBQ Brisket Tacos
- Kimchi Fried Rice with BBQ Pork
- Grilled Gochujang Chicken
- Spicy Korean BBQ Pork Skewers
- Bulgogi Lettuce Wraps
- Soy Garlic Ribeye Steak
- Kalbi Beef Tacos with Slaw
- Grilled Korean BBQ Chicken Wings
- Spicy Kimchi BBQ Burgers
- BBQ Pork Belly Sliders
- Grilled Gochujang Shrimp
- Korean BBQ Beef Skewers
- Dak Galbi (Spicy Stir-fried Chicken)
- Spicy Pork Bulgogi
- Galbi Jjim (Braised Short Ribs)
- Spicy Korean BBQ Tofu
- Pork Belly Kimchi Fried Rice
- Korean BBQ Meatballs
- Dak Bulgogi (Korean BBQ Chicken)
- Korean BBQ Pork Lettuce Wraps
- Kimchi BBQ Grilled Cheese
- Gochujang BBQ Salmon
- Spicy Pork BBQ Nachos
- Grilled Korean BBQ Eggplant
- BBQ Pork Belly Banh Mi
- Bulgogi Beef Bibimbap
- Korean BBQ Pork Stir-fry
- Spicy Grilled Tofu Skewers
- Gochujang BBQ Spare Ribs
- Korean BBQ Beef Sliders
- Spicy BBQ Pork Rice Bowls
- Soy Ginger Grilled Steak
- Korean BBQ Chicken Pizza

- Gochujang BBQ Wings
- Korean BBQ Beef Tacos
- Spicy Pork BBQ Lettuce Cups
- Grilled Korean BBQ Cauliflower
- Kimchi BBQ Grilled Corn
- Spicy Pork BBQ Quesadillas
- Gochujang BBQ Meatloaf
- Korean BBQ Beef Wraps
- Spicy Korean BBQ Potato Salad
- Soy Garlic BBQ Shrimp
- Korean BBQ Pulled Pork Sandwiches
- Grilled Gochujang Mushrooms
- Gochujang BBQ Beef Skewers
- Spicy Korean BBQ Brisket Sliders
- BBQ Kimchi Fried Rice Balls

Korean Beef Short Ribs (Galbi)

Ingredients:

- 3 pounds beef short ribs, cut across the bone (flanken style)
- 1 cup soy sauce
- 1/2 cup brown sugar
- 1/4 cup rice wine (mirin)
- 1/4 cup honey
- 1/4 cup sesame oil
- 6 cloves garlic, minced
- 1 small onion, grated
- 2 green onions, chopped
- 1 tablespoon sesame seeds
- 1/2 teaspoon black pepper
- Optional: sliced Asian pear or kiwi (for tenderizing, if desired)

Instructions:

1. Prepare the Marinade:
   - In a mixing bowl, combine soy sauce, brown sugar, rice wine (mirin), honey, sesame oil, minced garlic, grated onion, chopped green onions, sesame seeds, and black pepper. Mix well until the sugar is dissolved.
2. Marinate the Ribs:
   - Place the beef short ribs in a large resealable plastic bag or a shallow dish.
   - Pour the marinade over the ribs, ensuring they are fully coated. If using, add sliced Asian pear or kiwi to the marinade for additional tenderizing.
   - Seal the bag or cover the dish with plastic wrap and marinate in the refrigerator for at least 4 hours, preferably overnight. Turn the ribs occasionally to marinate evenly.
3. Grill the Ribs:
   - Preheat your grill to medium-high heat.
   - Remove the ribs from the marinade and shake off excess marinade.
   - Grill the ribs for about 3-4 minutes per side, or until nicely charred and cooked to your desired doneness. You can also cook them longer for well-done ribs.
4. Serve:
   - Transfer the grilled ribs to a serving plate.

- Garnish with additional chopped green onions and sesame seeds if desired.
- Serve hot with steamed rice, kimchi, and other Korean side dishes.

Enjoy your delicious Korean Beef Short Ribs (Galbi)!

Spicy Pork Belly (Samgyeopsal)

Ingredients:

- 1 pound pork belly, thinly sliced
- 3 tablespoons gochujang (Korean red chili paste)
- 2 tablespoons soy sauce
- 2 tablespoons honey or brown sugar
- 2 tablespoons mirin (rice wine)
- 3 cloves garlic, minced
- 1 tablespoon sesame oil
- 1 tablespoon sesame seeds
- 2 green onions, chopped (for garnish)
- Optional: sliced onion and green bell pepper

Instructions:

1. Prepare the Marinade:
    - In a mixing bowl, combine gochujang, soy sauce, honey (or brown sugar), mirin, minced garlic, sesame oil, and sesame seeds. Mix well until the marinade is smooth and well-combined.
2. Marinate the Pork Belly:
    - Place the thinly sliced pork belly in a large bowl or resealable plastic bag.
    - Pour the marinade over the pork belly, ensuring each slice is well-coated.
    - If time allows, marinate the pork belly for at least 30 minutes to 1 hour. For more flavor, marinate overnight in the refrigerator.
3. Cook the Spicy Pork Belly:
    - Heat a grill pan or skillet over medium-high heat.
    - Add the marinated pork belly slices to the pan, along with any optional sliced onion and green bell pepper.
    - Cook the pork belly slices for 3-4 minutes on each side, or until fully cooked and slightly caramelized.
4. Serve:
    - Transfer the cooked spicy pork belly to a serving plate.
    - Garnish with chopped green onions.
    - Serve hot with steamed rice, lettuce leaves (for wrapping), and other Korean side dishes like kimchi and pickled radishes.

Enjoy your homemade Spicy Pork Belly (Samgyeopsal)! This dish pairs perfectly with fresh lettuce wraps and a variety of Korean condiments for a delightful meal.

Korean BBQ Brisket Tacos

Ingredients:

For the Korean BBQ Brisket:

- 1 pound beef brisket, thinly sliced
- 1/2 cup soy sauce
- 1/4 cup brown sugar
- 2 tablespoons sesame oil
- 4 cloves garlic, minced
- 1 tablespoon ginger, grated
- 2 green onions, chopped
- 1 tablespoon sesame seeds
- 1 tablespoon rice vinegar
- 1 tablespoon gochujang (Korean red chili paste) (optional for spiciness)

For the Tacos:

- 8-10 small flour or corn tortillas
- Kimchi, for serving
- Sriracha or gochujang mayo (mix sriracha or gochujang with mayo), for topping
- Thinly sliced cabbage or lettuce
- Chopped cilantro, for garnish
- Lime wedges, for serving

Instructions:

1. Marinate the Brisket:
    - In a bowl, combine soy sauce, brown sugar, sesame oil, minced garlic, grated ginger, chopped green onions, sesame seeds, rice vinegar, and gochujang (if using). Mix well.
    - Place the thinly sliced beef brisket in a resealable plastic bag or shallow dish.
    - Pour the marinade over the brisket, making sure it's well-coated.
    - Marinate in the refrigerator for at least 1 hour, or preferably overnight.
2. Cook the Korean BBQ Brisket:
    - Heat a skillet or grill pan over medium-high heat.
    - Add the marinated brisket slices (reserve the marinade) and cook for 3-4 minutes on each side, or until cooked through and caramelized.

- If needed, you can also cook the brisket on an outdoor grill.
3. Warm the Tortillas:
    - Heat the tortillas in a dry skillet or microwave until warm and pliable.
4. Assemble the Tacos:
    - Place a few slices of Korean BBQ brisket on each tortilla.
    - Top with kimchi, thinly sliced cabbage or lettuce, and drizzle with sriracha or gochujang mayo.
    - Garnish with chopped cilantro and serve with lime wedges on the side.
5. Serve and Enjoy:
    - Serve the Korean BBQ Brisket Tacos immediately.
    - Enjoy these flavorful tacos with a burst of Korean BBQ goodness!

These Korean BBQ Brisket Tacos are perfect for a delicious and unique meal that combines the best of Korean and Mexican flavors. Adjust the spiciness according to your preference and enjoy!

Kimchi Fried Rice with BBQ Pork

Ingredients:

- 2 cups cooked rice (preferably day-old rice)
- 1 cup kimchi, chopped
- 1/2 cup cooked BBQ pork (or leftover grilled pork), diced
- 2 tablespoons kimchi juice (from the kimchi jar)
- 2 tablespoons soy sauce
- 1 tablespoon sesame oil
- 2 green onions, chopped
- 2 cloves garlic, minced
- 1 tablespoon vegetable oil
- Optional: fried egg for topping
- Sesame seeds, for garnish

Instructions:

1. Prepare Ingredients:
    - Ensure your rice is cooked and cooled. Day-old rice works best for fried rice.
    - Chop the kimchi into small pieces.
    - Dice the cooked BBQ pork into small cubes.
    - Chop the green onions, separating the white and green parts.
2. Stir-Fry Kimchi and Pork:
    - Heat vegetable oil in a large skillet or wok over medium-high heat.
    - Add the minced garlic and the white parts of the green onions. Sauté for about 30 seconds until fragrant.
    - Add the chopped kimchi and diced BBQ pork to the skillet. Stir-fry for 2-3 minutes until heated through.
3. Add Rice and Seasoning:
    - Add the cooked rice to the skillet, breaking up any clumps with a spatula.
    - Drizzle soy sauce and sesame oil over the rice.
    - Pour in the kimchi juice from the kimchi jar. Stir well to combine all ingredients evenly.
4. Cook Kimchi Fried Rice:
    - Continue stir-frying the rice mixture for 5-6 minutes, or until the rice is heated through and slightly crispy.
    - Taste and adjust seasoning if needed (add more soy sauce or sesame oil according to your preference).

5. Serve Kimchi Fried Rice:
    - Remove the skillet from heat.
    - Garnish the kimchi fried rice with the remaining chopped green onions and sesame seeds.
    - Optionally, top each serving with a fried egg for extra richness and flavor.
6. Enjoy Your Meal:
    - Divide the kimchi fried rice into bowls or plates.
    - Serve hot as a main dish or side dish. Enjoy the delicious blend of flavors!

This Kimchi Fried Rice with BBQ Pork is a delightful dish that's perfect for using leftover rice and BBQ pork. The kimchi adds a wonderful tangy kick, making this fried rice both comforting and uniquely flavorful. Adjust the spice level by adding more or less kimchi according to your taste preferences.

Grilled Gochujang Chicken

Ingredients:

- 4 boneless, skinless chicken breasts
- 3 tablespoons gochujang (Korean red chili paste)
- 2 tablespoons soy sauce
- 2 tablespoons honey
- 2 tablespoons rice vinegar
- 2 cloves garlic, minced
- 1 tablespoon sesame oil
- 1 tablespoon grated ginger
- 1 tablespoon vegetable oil (for grilling)
- Sesame seeds and chopped green onions, for garnish

Instructions:

1. Prepare the Marinade:
    - In a mixing bowl, combine gochujang, soy sauce, honey, rice vinegar, minced garlic, sesame oil, and grated ginger. Mix well until the marinade is smooth.
2. Marinate the Chicken:
    - Place the chicken breasts in a resealable plastic bag or shallow dish.
    - Pour the marinade over the chicken, ensuring each piece is well-coated.
    - Seal the bag or cover the dish with plastic wrap.
    - Marinate in the refrigerator for at least 1 hour, or ideally overnight for maximum flavor.
3. Preheat the Grill:
    - Preheat your grill to medium-high heat.
    - Brush the grill grates with vegetable oil to prevent sticking.
4. Grill the Chicken:
    - Remove the chicken from the marinade, allowing excess marinade to drip off.
    - Place the chicken breasts on the preheated grill.
    - Grill for 6-8 minutes per side, or until the chicken is cooked through and has nice grill marks. The internal temperature should reach 165°F (75°C).
5. Rest and Serve:
    - Once cooked, transfer the grilled chicken to a plate and let it rest for a few minutes.
    - Slice the chicken breasts into thin strips or serve them whole.

- Garnish with sesame seeds and chopped green onions.
6. Serve Grilled Gochujang Chicken:
    - Arrange the grilled chicken on a serving platter.
    - Serve hot with steamed rice and your favorite Korean side dishes like kimchi, pickled vegetables, or a fresh salad.

Enjoy your flavorful and spicy Grilled Gochujang Chicken! This dish is perfect for a delicious and satisfying meal that showcases the bold flavors of Korean cuisine. Adjust the level of spiciness by adding more or less gochujang according to your preference.

Spicy Korean BBQ Pork Skewers

Ingredients:

- 1 pound pork tenderloin or pork shoulder, cut into cubes
- 2 tablespoons gochujang (Korean red chili paste)
- 2 tablespoons soy sauce
- 2 tablespoons honey
- 2 tablespoons sesame oil
- 4 cloves garlic, minced
- 1 tablespoon grated ginger
- 1 tablespoon rice vinegar
- 1 tablespoon sesame seeds
- 2 green onions, chopped (for garnish)
- Wooden skewers, soaked in water for 30 minutes

Instructions:

1. Prepare the Marinade:
    - In a mixing bowl, combine gochujang, soy sauce, honey, sesame oil, minced garlic, grated ginger, rice vinegar, and sesame seeds. Mix well until the marinade is smooth.
2. Marinate the Pork:
    - Place the cubed pork in a shallow dish or resealable plastic bag.
    - Pour the marinade over the pork, making sure all pieces are well-coated.
    - Cover the dish or seal the bag, and marinate in the refrigerator for at least 1 hour, or ideally overnight for maximum flavor.
3. Skewer the Pork:
    - Preheat your grill or broiler.
    - Thread the marinated pork cubes onto the soaked wooden skewers, dividing them evenly.
4. Grill or Broil the Skewers:
    - If using a grill, preheat it to medium-high heat.
    - Place the skewers on the grill or under the broiler.
    - Cook for 4-5 minutes on each side, or until the pork is cooked through and nicely caramelized. Turn the skewers occasionally to ensure even cooking.
5. Serve the Skewers:
    - Once cooked, transfer the spicy Korean BBQ pork skewers to a serving platter.
    - Garnish with chopped green onions.

- Serve hot as an appetizer or main dish.
6. Enjoy Your Spicy Korean BBQ Pork Skewers:
    - Serve the skewers with steamed rice and your favorite Korean side dishes such as kimchi, pickled vegetables, or a fresh salad.

These Spicy Korean BBQ Pork Skewers are perfect for grilling outdoors or broiling indoors. The marinade infuses the pork with bold and spicy flavors, creating a delicious and memorable dish that everyone will love. Adjust the level of spiciness by adding more or less gochujang according to your preference.

Bulgogi Lettuce Wraps

Ingredients:

For the Bulgogi Marinade:

- 1 pound beef sirloin or rib eye, thinly sliced
- 1/2 cup soy sauce
- 3 tablespoons brown sugar
- 3 tablespoons sesame oil
- 4 cloves garlic, minced
- 1 tablespoon grated ginger
- 2 tablespoons rice vinegar
- 2 tablespoons mirin (rice wine)
- 2 green onions, chopped
- 1 tablespoon sesame seeds
- Freshly ground black pepper, to taste

For Serving:

- Butter lettuce leaves (or any lettuce of your choice)
- Cooked rice
- Sliced cucumber
- Sliced carrots
- Sliced green onions
- Kimchi
- Gochujang (Korean red chili paste), optional for extra spice

Instructions:

1. Prepare the Bulgogi Marinade:
    - In a bowl, whisk together soy sauce, brown sugar, sesame oil, minced garlic, grated ginger, rice vinegar, mirin, chopped green onions, sesame seeds, and black pepper.
2. Marinate the Beef:
    - Place the thinly sliced beef in a bowl or resealable plastic bag.
    - Pour the bulgogi marinade over the beef, ensuring each slice is coated.
    - Marinate in the refrigerator for at least 1 hour, or ideally overnight for maximum flavor.
3. Cook the Bulgogi:

- Heat a large skillet or grill pan over medium-high heat.
- Add the marinated beef slices to the skillet, reserving any excess marinade.
- Cook the beef for 3-4 minutes, stirring occasionally, until cooked through and caramelized. You may need to cook in batches to avoid overcrowding the pan.

4. Assemble the Lettuce Wraps:
   - Arrange the butter lettuce leaves on a serving platter.
   - Place a spoonful of cooked rice on each lettuce leaf.
   - Top with a few slices of the cooked bulgogi.
5. Add Toppings:
   - Garnish the bulgogi lettuce wraps with sliced cucumber, carrots, green onions, and kimchi.
   - Drizzle with additional marinade or gochujang for extra flavor and spice.
6. Serve and Enjoy:
   - Serve the bulgogi lettuce wraps immediately as a delicious and healthy meal or appetizer.
   - To eat, wrap the lettuce leaf around the bulgogi and toppings, and enjoy the flavorful combination of textures and flavors.

Bulgogi Lettuce Wraps are a delightful way to enjoy Korean barbecue flavors in a fresh and light dish. Customize the toppings and spice level according to your preference, and savor the deliciousness of this Korean-inspired meal!

Soy Garlic Ribeye Steak

Ingredients:

- 2 ribeye steaks, about 1-inch thick
- 1/3 cup soy sauce
- 1/4 cup brown sugar
- 4 cloves garlic, minced
- 2 tablespoons sesame oil
- 2 tablespoons rice vinegar
- 1 tablespoon grated ginger
- 1/2 teaspoon black pepper
- 2 green onions, chopped (for garnish)
- 1 tablespoon vegetable oil (for cooking)

Instructions:

1. Prepare the Marinade:
    - In a bowl, whisk together soy sauce, brown sugar, minced garlic, sesame oil, rice vinegar, grated ginger, and black pepper until the sugar is dissolved.
2. Marinate the Ribeye Steaks:
    - Place the ribeye steaks in a shallow dish or resealable plastic bag.
    - Pour the marinade over the steaks, ensuring they are well-coated.
    - Marinate in the refrigerator for at least 1 hour, or preferably up to 4 hours for maximum flavor. Turn the steaks occasionally to marinate evenly.
3. Cook the Ribeye Steaks:
    - Remove the marinated ribeye steaks from the refrigerator and let them come to room temperature for about 30 minutes before cooking.
    - Heat a grill pan, cast iron skillet, or outdoor grill over medium-high heat.
    - Brush the cooking surface with vegetable oil to prevent sticking.
    - Remove the steaks from the marinade (reserve the marinade for basting) and pat them dry with paper towels.
    - Place the steaks on the hot grill or skillet.
    - Cook the steaks for about 4-5 minutes on each side for medium-rare, or adjust cooking time according to desired doneness.
    - During cooking, baste the steaks with the reserved marinade using a brush.
4. Rest and Serve:

- Once cooked to your liking, remove the ribeye steaks from the heat and let them rest for 5-10 minutes on a cutting board. This allows the juices to redistribute.
5. Slice and Garnish:
    - Slice the ribeye steaks against the grain into thin strips.
    - Arrange the sliced steaks on a serving platter.
    - Garnish with chopped green onions.
6. Serve and Enjoy:
    - Serve the Soy Garlic Ribeye Steak hot with steamed rice, roasted vegetables, or a fresh salad.
    - Enjoy the tender and flavorful ribeye steak infused with soy garlic goodness!

This Soy Garlic Ribeye Steak recipe is perfect for a special dinner at home. The marinade adds depth of flavor to the ribeye steak, making it irresistibly delicious and satisfying. Adjust the cooking time based on the thickness of your steaks and your preferred level of doneness.

Kalbi Beef Tacos with Slaw

Ingredients:

For the Kalbi Beef:

- 1.5 pounds beef short ribs, thinly sliced across the bone (flanken style)
- 1/2 cup soy sauce
- 1/4 cup brown sugar
- 2 tablespoons sesame oil
- 4 cloves garlic, minced
- 1 tablespoon grated ginger
- 2 green onions, chopped
- 1 tablespoon rice vinegar
- 1 tablespoon sesame seeds
- Freshly ground black pepper, to taste

For the Slaw:

- 2 cups shredded cabbage (green or purple)
- 1 carrot, julienned or grated
- 2 green onions, thinly sliced
- 1/4 cup mayonnaise
- 1 tablespoon rice vinegar
- 1 teaspoon sugar
- Salt and pepper, to taste

For Serving:

- Flour or corn tortillas
- Sriracha or gochujang mayo (optional)
- Fresh cilantro, chopped (for garnish)

Instructions:

1. Prepare the Kalbi Beef Marinade:
    - In a bowl, whisk together soy sauce, brown sugar, sesame oil, minced garlic, grated ginger, chopped green onions, rice vinegar, sesame seeds, and black pepper.

2. Marinate the Beef:
   - Place the thinly sliced beef short ribs in a shallow dish or resealable plastic bag.
   - Pour the marinade over the beef, ensuring all pieces are coated.
   - Marinate in the refrigerator for at least 2 hours, or ideally overnight for maximum flavor.
3. Make the Slaw:
   - In a bowl, combine shredded cabbage, julienned/grated carrot, and thinly sliced green onions.
   - In a separate small bowl, whisk together mayonnaise, rice vinegar, sugar, salt, and pepper.
   - Pour the dressing over the cabbage mixture and toss until well combined. Adjust seasoning to taste.
4. Cook the Kalbi Beef:
   - Heat a grill or grill pan over medium-high heat.
   - Remove the marinated beef from the refrigerator and let excess marinade drip off.
   - Grill the beef slices for 2-3 minutes on each side, or until cooked to your desired doneness and caramelized.
5. Assemble the Tacos:
   - Warm the tortillas in a dry skillet or microwave.
   - Place a few slices of grilled Kalbi beef on each tortilla.
   - Top with a generous amount of slaw.
   - Drizzle with sriracha or gochujang mayo (if using) for extra spice.
   - Garnish with chopped cilantro.
6. Serve and Enjoy:
   - Serve the Kalbi Beef Tacos immediately.
   - Enjoy the delicious fusion of Korean flavors in a taco form!

These Kalbi Beef Tacos with Slaw are perfect for a casual dinner or party. The tender marinated beef combined with crunchy slaw and soft tortillas create a delightful taste experience. Customize the toppings and spiciness according to your preference, and enjoy these flavorful tacos with family and friends!

Grilled Korean BBQ Chicken Wings

Ingredients:

- 2 pounds chicken wings, tips removed and separated into flats and drumettes
- 1/2 cup soy sauce
- 1/4 cup brown sugar
- 2 tablespoons sesame oil
- 4 cloves garlic, minced
- 1 tablespoon grated ginger
- 2 tablespoons rice vinegar
- 2 tablespoons gochujang (Korean red chili paste)
- 2 green onions, chopped (for garnish)
- Sesame seeds, for garnish
- Vegetable oil, for grilling

Instructions:

1. Prepare the Marinade:
    - In a bowl, combine soy sauce, brown sugar, sesame oil, minced garlic, grated ginger, rice vinegar, and gochujang. Mix well until the sugar is dissolved and the marinade is smooth.
2. Marinate the Chicken Wings:
    - Place the chicken wings in a large resealable plastic bag or a shallow dish.
    - Pour the marinade over the chicken wings, ensuring they are well-coated.
    - Marinate in the refrigerator for at least 2 hours, or ideally overnight for maximum flavor.
3. Preheat the Grill:
    - Preheat your grill to medium-high heat.
    - Brush the grill grates with vegetable oil to prevent sticking.
4. Grill the Chicken Wings:
    - Remove the chicken wings from the marinade, allowing excess marinade to drip off.
    - Place the chicken wings on the preheated grill.
    - Grill the chicken wings for about 15-20 minutes, turning occasionally, until they are cooked through and nicely charred.
5. Garnish and Serve:
    - Transfer the grilled chicken wings to a serving platter.
    - Garnish with chopped green onions and sesame seeds.
6. Serve and Enjoy:

- Serve the Grilled Korean BBQ Chicken Wings hot as an appetizer or main dish.
- Enjoy the delicious flavors of Korean barbecue with these tender and flavorful chicken wings!

These Grilled Korean BBQ Chicken Wings are perfect for a barbecue party or a weeknight dinner. Serve them with steamed rice, kimchi, and other Korean side dishes for a complete meal. Adjust the amount of gochujang according to your spice preference. These wings are sure to be a hit with family and friends!

Spicy Kimchi BBQ Burgers

Ingredients:

For the Kimchi BBQ Sauce:

- 1 cup kimchi, chopped
- 1/2 cup ketchup
- 2 tablespoons gochujang (Korean red chili paste)
- 2 tablespoons soy sauce
- 2 tablespoons brown sugar
- 1 tablespoon rice vinegar
- 2 cloves garlic, minced
- 1 tablespoon sesame oil

For the Burgers:

- 1 pound ground beef (preferably 80% lean)
- Salt and pepper, to taste
- 4 hamburger buns
- Sliced cheese (optional)
- Additional kimchi, for topping
- Lettuce leaves
- Sliced onions (optional)
- Sliced tomatoes (optional)

Instructions:

1. Make the Kimchi BBQ Sauce:
    - In a blender or food processor, combine chopped kimchi, ketchup, gochujang, soy sauce, brown sugar, rice vinegar, minced garlic, and sesame oil.
    - Blend until smooth. If needed, add a little water to achieve desired consistency. Set aside.
2. Prepare the Burgers:
    - Preheat your grill or skillet over medium-high heat.
    - Season the ground beef with salt and pepper in a bowl.
    - Divide the seasoned beef into 4 equal portions and shape them into burger patties.
3. Cook the Burgers:

- Grill or cook the burger patties for about 4-5 minutes per side, or until they reach your desired level of doneness.
- During the last minute of cooking, brush each burger patty with the prepared Kimchi BBQ Sauce, allowing it to caramelize slightly.

4. Assemble the Burgers:
   - Toast the hamburger buns on the grill or in a toaster.
   - Place a burger patty on the bottom half of each bun.
   - Top each patty with a slice of cheese (if using), additional kimchi, lettuce leaves, sliced onions, and tomatoes.
5. Serve and Enjoy:
   - Close the burgers with the top halves of the buns.
   - Serve the Spicy Kimchi BBQ Burgers immediately.
   - Enjoy the delicious combination of flavors and textures in every bite!

These Spicy Kimchi BBQ Burgers are sure to be a hit at your next barbecue or casual dinner. The tangy and spicy kimchi BBQ sauce adds a unique twist to traditional burgers, making them incredibly flavorful and satisfying. Customize the toppings and spice level according to your preference, and enjoy these mouthwatering burgers with family and friends!

BBQ Pork Belly Sliders

Ingredients:

For the Pork Belly:

- 1 pound pork belly, skin removed and cut into small slices or cubes
- Salt and pepper, to taste
- 1 cup barbecue sauce (homemade or store-bought)

For the Sliders:

- Mini slider buns or dinner rolls
- Coleslaw (optional, for topping)
- Pickles (optional, for topping)
- Sliced red onions (optional, for topping)

Instructions:

1. Preheat the Oven:
    - Preheat your oven to 350°F (175°C).
2. Prepare the Pork Belly:
    - Season the pork belly slices or cubes with salt and pepper.
3. Cook the Pork Belly:
    - Heat a skillet or oven-safe pan over medium-high heat.
    - Sear the pork belly pieces on all sides until browned and crispy (about 2-3 minutes per side).
    - Remove excess fat from the skillet, if necessary.
    - Pour the barbecue sauce over the pork belly and toss to coat evenly.
4. Bake the Pork Belly:
    - Transfer the skillet or pan to the preheated oven.
    - Bake for 45-60 minutes, or until the pork belly is tender and caramelized, basting with the barbecue sauce halfway through cooking.
5. Assemble the Sliders:
    - Slice the slider buns or dinner rolls in half.
    - Place a spoonful of BBQ pork belly onto the bottom half of each bun.
    - Top with coleslaw, pickles, sliced red onions, or your favorite toppings.
6. Serve and Enjoy:
    - Close the sliders with the top halves of the buns.

- Secure each slider with a toothpick if needed.
- Serve the BBQ Pork Belly Sliders immediately, and enjoy this delicious and satisfying appetizer or main dish!

These BBQ Pork Belly Sliders are perfect for parties, game days, or casual gatherings. The tender and flavorful pork belly combined with barbecue sauce and your favorite toppings makes these sliders irresistibly delicious. Customize the sliders with different toppings to suit your taste preferences, and watch them disappear from the plate!

Grilled Gochujang Shrimp

Ingredients:

- 1 pound large shrimp, peeled and deveined
- 3 tablespoons gochujang (Korean red chili paste)
- 2 tablespoons soy sauce
- 2 tablespoons honey
- 2 tablespoons sesame oil
- 2 cloves garlic, minced
- 1 tablespoon grated ginger
- 1 tablespoon rice vinegar
- 1 tablespoon sesame seeds
- Sliced green onions, for garnish
- Lime wedges, for serving

Instructions:

1. Prepare the Gochujang Marinade:
    - In a bowl, combine gochujang, soy sauce, honey, sesame oil, minced garlic, grated ginger, rice vinegar, and sesame seeds. Mix well to create a smooth marinade.
2. Marinate the Shrimp:
    - Place the peeled and deveined shrimp in a shallow dish or resealable plastic bag.
    - Pour the gochujang marinade over the shrimp, ensuring all shrimp are coated evenly.
    - Cover the dish or seal the bag, and marinate in the refrigerator for at least 30 minutes, or up to 2 hours.
3. Preheat the Grill:
    - Preheat your grill to medium-high heat.
4. Skewer the Shrimp (optional):
    - If using wooden skewers, soak them in water for 30 minutes to prevent burning.
    - Thread the marinated shrimp onto skewers for easier grilling, or grill the shrimp directly on the grill grates.
5. Grill the Shrimp:
    - Place the shrimp skewers or directly on the grill grates.
    - Grill for 2-3 minutes on each side, or until the shrimp are pink and opaque, and slightly charred.

6. Serve and Garnish:
    - Remove the grilled shrimp from the grill and transfer to a serving platter.
    - Garnish with sliced green onions.
    - Serve hot with lime wedges on the side for squeezing over the shrimp.
7. Enjoy Your Grilled Gochujang Shrimp:
    - Serve the grilled shrimp as an appetizer or main dish.
    - Enjoy the spicy, savory, and slightly sweet flavors of the gochujang marinade with perfectly grilled shrimp!

Grilled Gochujang Shrimp is perfect for summer barbecues or as a delicious appetizer for any occasion. The marinade adds a delightful Korean-inspired twist to grilled shrimp, making it a flavorful and impressive dish that's sure to be a hit! Adjust the spice level by adding more or less gochujang according to your preference.

Korean BBQ Beef Skewers

Ingredients:

- 1.5 pounds beef sirloin or ribeye, thinly sliced against the grain
- 1/2 cup soy sauce
- 1/4 cup brown sugar
- 3 tablespoons sesame oil
- 4 cloves garlic, minced
- 2 tablespoons grated ginger
- 2 tablespoons rice vinegar
- 2 green onions, finely chopped
- 1 tablespoon sesame seeds
- Freshly ground black pepper, to taste
- Wooden skewers, soaked in water for 30 minutes

Instructions:

1. Prepare the Marinade:
    - In a bowl, combine soy sauce, brown sugar, sesame oil, minced garlic, grated ginger, rice vinegar, chopped green onions, sesame seeds, and black pepper. Mix well until the sugar is dissolved.
2. Marinate the Beef:
    - Place the thinly sliced beef in a shallow dish or resealable plastic bag.
    - Pour the marinade over the beef, ensuring all pieces are well-coated.
    - Cover the dish or seal the bag, and marinate in the refrigerator for at least 1 hour, or ideally overnight for maximum flavor.
3. Skewer the Beef:
    - Preheat your grill or grill pan over medium-high heat.
    - Thread the marinated beef slices onto the soaked wooden skewers, dividing evenly and leaving a small space between each piece.
4. Grill the Skewers:
    - Brush the grill grates with oil to prevent sticking.
    - Place the beef skewers on the preheated grill.
    - Grill for about 3-4 minutes on each side, or until the beef is cooked to your desired level of doneness and has nice grill marks.
5. Serve and Enjoy:
    - Remove the grilled beef skewers from the heat.
    - Serve hot with steamed rice and Korean side dishes like kimchi, pickled vegetables, or fresh salad.

- Garnish with extra chopped green onions and sesame seeds, if desired.
6. Optional Sauce:
    - If desired, serve the beef skewers with a side of gochujang-based dipping sauce for extra flavor and spice.

Enjoy these delicious Korean BBQ Beef Skewers as a main dish or appetizer at your next gathering. The flavorful marinade combined with the charred, juicy beef makes these skewers a crowd-pleaser that's perfect for grilling season! Adjust the marinade ingredients to suit your taste preferences and enjoy the authentic Korean BBQ experience at home.

Dak Galbi (Spicy Stir-fried Chicken)

Ingredients:

- 1 pound boneless, skinless chicken thighs or breast, thinly sliced
- 2 cups cabbage, thinly sliced
- 1 small onion, thinly sliced
- 1 sweet potato, peeled and thinly sliced
- 1 carrot, thinly sliced
- 4-5 perilla leaves (optional), thinly sliced
- 3-4 tablespoons vegetable oil

For the Marinade:

- 3 tablespoons gochujang (Korean red chili paste)
- 2 tablespoons soy sauce
- 1 tablespoon honey or brown sugar
- 1 tablespoon sesame oil
- 3 cloves garlic, minced
- 1 tablespoon grated ginger
- 1 tablespoon rice wine or mirin
- 1 teaspoon Korean red chili powder (gochugaru), adjust to taste
- Salt and pepper, to taste

For Serving (optional):

- Cooked rice
- Lettuce leaves or perilla leaves for wrapping

Instructions:

1. Prepare the Marinade:
    - In a bowl, whisk together gochujang, soy sauce, honey or brown sugar, sesame oil, minced garlic, grated ginger, rice wine or mirin, Korean red chili powder (gochugaru), salt, and pepper. Adjust seasoning to taste.
2. Marinate the Chicken:
    - Place the thinly sliced chicken in a bowl.
    - Pour the marinade over the chicken and mix well to coat.
    - Let the chicken marinate for at least 30 minutes, or ideally 1-2 hours in the refrigerator.

3. Prepare the Vegetables:
   - Slice the cabbage, onion, sweet potato, carrot, and perilla leaves (if using) into thin strips.
4. Stir-fry the Chicken and Vegetables:
   - Heat 2 tablespoons of vegetable oil in a large skillet or wok over medium-high heat.
   - Add the marinated chicken and stir-fry for 5-6 minutes until the chicken is almost cooked through.
5. Add the Vegetables:
   - Push the chicken to one side of the skillet.
   - Add the remaining 1-2 tablespoons of vegetable oil to the empty side of the skillet.
   - Add the sliced cabbage, onion, sweet potato, carrot, and perilla leaves (if using) to the skillet.
   - Stir-fry the vegetables for about 5-6 minutes until they start to soften.
6. Combine and Finish Cooking:
   - Mix the chicken and vegetables together in the skillet.
   - Stir-fry for an additional 3-4 minutes until the chicken is fully cooked and the vegetables are tender-crisp.
7. Serve Dak Galbi:
   - Transfer the Dak Galbi to a serving platter.
   - Serve hot with cooked rice and lettuce leaves or perilla leaves for wrapping.
   - Enjoy this spicy and flavorful Dak Galbi with your favorite side dishes!

Dak Galbi is a delicious and satisfying Korean dish that's perfect for sharing with family and friends. Adjust the spiciness level by adding more or less Korean red chili powder (gochugaru) according to your preference. Serve with rice and wrap the stir-fried chicken and vegetables in lettuce or perilla leaves for a delightful Korean dining experience!

Spicy Pork Bulgogi

Ingredients:

- 1 pound pork shoulder or pork loin, thinly sliced
- 4 cloves garlic, minced
- 2 tablespoons gochujang (Korean red chili paste)
- 2 tablespoons soy sauce
- 1 tablespoon sesame oil
- 1 tablespoon honey or brown sugar
- 1 tablespoon rice wine or mirin
- 1 tablespoon grated ginger
- 2 green onions, chopped (for garnish)
- 1 tablespoon vegetable oil, for cooking
- Sesame seeds, for garnish (optional)
- Cooked rice, for serving
- Lettuce leaves or perilla leaves, for wrapping (optional)

Instructions:

1. Prepare the Marinade:
    - In a bowl, combine minced garlic, gochujang, soy sauce, sesame oil, honey or brown sugar, rice wine or mirin, and grated ginger. Mix well to make the marinade.
2. Marinate the Pork:
    - Place the thinly sliced pork in a bowl or resealable plastic bag.
    - Pour the marinade over the pork, ensuring all slices are well-coated.
    - Cover the bowl or seal the bag, and marinate in the refrigerator for at least 1 hour, or ideally 2-3 hours for maximum flavor.
3. Cook the Spicy Pork Bulgogi:
    - Heat vegetable oil in a large skillet or wok over medium-high heat.
    - Add the marinated pork (including the marinade) to the skillet.
    - Stir-fry the pork for 5-6 minutes, or until the pork is fully cooked and caramelized, and the sauce has thickened slightly.
4. Garnish and Serve:
    - Garnish the Spicy Pork Bulgogi with chopped green onions and sesame seeds (if using).
    - Serve hot with cooked rice.
    - Optionally, serve with lettuce leaves or perilla leaves for wrapping the spicy pork.

5. Enjoy Spicy Pork Bulgogi:
   - Serve the Spicy Pork Bulgogi as a main dish with rice and side dishes, or wrap the pork in lettuce or perilla leaves for a Korean-style wrap.
   - Enjoy the delicious and spicy flavors of this classic Korean dish!

Spicy Pork Bulgogi is perfect for a weeknight dinner or as part of a Korean-inspired meal spread. Adjust the level of spiciness by adding more or less gochujang according to your taste preferences. Serve with steamed rice and your favorite Korean side dishes for a complete and satisfying meal!

Galbi Jjim (Braised Short Ribs)

Ingredients:

- 2 pounds beef short ribs, cut into 3-inch pieces
- 1 large onion, sliced
- 4 cloves garlic, minced
- 2 tablespoons soy sauce
- 2 tablespoons brown sugar
- 2 tablespoons honey
- 1 tablespoon sesame oil
- 1 tablespoon rice wine or mirin
- 1 tablespoon sesame seeds
- 1 teaspoon black pepper
- 2 cups water or beef broth
- 2 carrots, peeled and cut into chunks
- 1 large potato, peeled and cut into chunks
- 4-5 shiitake mushrooms, sliced (optional)
- 2 green onions, chopped (for garnish)
- Steamed rice, for serving

Instructions:

1. Prepare the Short Ribs:
    - Rinse the beef short ribs under cold water and pat them dry with paper towels.
    - Cut the short ribs into 3-inch pieces, if they are not already cut.
2. Make the Braising Sauce:
    - In a bowl, combine minced garlic, soy sauce, brown sugar, honey, sesame oil, rice wine or mirin, sesame seeds, and black pepper. Mix well to make the braising sauce.
3. Braise the Short Ribs:
    - Heat a large pot or Dutch oven over medium-high heat.
    - Add the sliced onion to the pot and sauté for 2-3 minutes until softened.
    - Add the beef short ribs to the pot and sear them on all sides until browned.
4. Add Braising Sauce and Liquid:
    - Pour the prepared braising sauce over the short ribs in the pot.
    - Add 2 cups of water or beef broth to the pot, enough to cover the short ribs.

- Bring the liquid to a simmer.
5. Simmer and Cook:
    - Cover the pot with a lid and reduce the heat to low.
    - Let the short ribs simmer for 1.5 to 2 hours, or until the meat is tender and falling off the bone.
    - Stir occasionally and add more water or broth if needed to keep the short ribs covered with liquid.
6. Add Vegetables:
    - After the short ribs have simmered for about 1 hour, add the carrots, potatoes, and sliced shiitake mushrooms (if using) to the pot.
    - Continue to simmer for another 30-45 minutes, or until the vegetables are tender and cooked through.
7. Serve Galbi Jjim:
    - Once the short ribs and vegetables are cooked, transfer them to a serving platter.
    - Garnish with chopped green onions.
    - Serve hot with steamed rice.
8. Enjoy Galbi Jjim:
    - Serve the Galbi Jjim as a hearty and comforting Korean meal.
    - Enjoy the tender and flavorful braised short ribs with the savory sauce and vegetables!

Galbi Jjim is a comforting and satisfying dish that's perfect for special occasions or family gatherings. The slow braising process allows the meat to become incredibly tender and infused with the delicious flavors of the sauce. Serve this dish with steamed rice and enjoy the authentic taste of Korean cuisine!

Spicy Korean BBQ Tofu

Ingredients:

- 1 block (14-16 ounces) firm tofu
- 2 tablespoons soy sauce
- 2 tablespoons gochujang (Korean red chili paste)
- 1 tablespoon sesame oil
- 1 tablespoon honey or brown sugar
- 2 cloves garlic, minced
- 1 tablespoon rice vinegar
- 1 tablespoon sesame seeds
- 2 green onions, chopped (for garnish)
- 1 tablespoon vegetable oil, for cooking
- Cooked rice, for serving
- Steamed vegetables, for serving (optional)

Instructions:

1. Prepare the Tofu:
    - Drain the tofu and wrap it in paper towels.
    - Place a heavy object (such as a plate or skillet) on top of the wrapped tofu to press out excess moisture for about 15-20 minutes.
    - Unwrap the tofu and cut it into cubes or slices.
2. Make the Korean BBQ Sauce:
    - In a bowl, whisk together soy sauce, gochujang, sesame oil, honey or brown sugar, minced garlic, rice vinegar, and sesame seeds. Adjust the sweetness and spiciness according to your taste.
3. Marinate the Tofu:
    - Place the tofu cubes in a shallow dish or bowl.
    - Pour half of the Korean BBQ sauce over the tofu, reserving the other half for later.
    - Gently toss the tofu to coat evenly with the marinade.
    - Let the tofu marinate for at least 15-20 minutes to absorb the flavors.
4. Cook the Tofu:
    - Heat vegetable oil in a non-stick skillet or wok over medium-high heat.
    - Add the marinated tofu cubes to the skillet in a single layer.
    - Cook the tofu for 4-5 minutes, flipping occasionally, until all sides are golden brown and crispy.
5. Add Remaining Sauce:

- Pour the remaining Korean BBQ sauce over the cooked tofu in the skillet.
- Stir gently to coat the tofu with the sauce.
- Allow the sauce to simmer for 1-2 minutes, until it thickens slightly and coats the tofu.

6. Serve Spicy Korean BBQ Tofu:
    - Transfer the spicy tofu to a serving dish.
    - Garnish with chopped green onions.
    - Serve hot with steamed rice and your choice of steamed vegetables.
7. Enjoy Your Spicy Korean BBQ Tofu:
    - Serve the Spicy Korean BBQ Tofu as a main dish or part of a Korean-inspired meal.
    - Enjoy the crispy tofu cubes coated in a delicious and spicy barbecue sauce!

This Spicy Korean BBQ Tofu is a great vegetarian option packed with bold flavors. Customize the level of spiciness by adjusting the amount of gochujang and enjoy this dish with rice and veggies for a satisfying and tasty meal!

Pork Belly Kimchi Fried Rice

Ingredients:

- 1 cup cooked rice (preferably day-old rice)
- 200 grams pork belly, thinly sliced
- 1 cup kimchi, chopped
- 2 cloves garlic, minced
- 2 green onions, chopped
- 2 eggs
- 1 tablespoon soy sauce
- 1 tablespoon gochujang (Korean red chili paste)
- 1 tablespoon sesame oil
- 1 tablespoon vegetable oil
- Salt and pepper, to taste
- Sesame seeds, for garnish (optional)

Instructions:

1. Prepare the Ingredients:
    - If you don't have cooked rice ready, cook rice in advance and let it cool before using for fried rice.
    - Thinly slice the pork belly into bite-sized pieces.
    - Chop the kimchi into small pieces.
    - Mince the garlic and chop the green onions.
2. Marinate the Pork Belly:
    - In a bowl, combine the sliced pork belly with soy sauce and gochujang. Mix well to coat the pork evenly. Let it marinate for about 10-15 minutes.
3. Cook the Pork Belly:
    - Heat vegetable oil in a large skillet or wok over medium-high heat.
    - Add the marinated pork belly to the skillet and cook until it's crispy and golden brown, about 5-7 minutes.
    - Remove the pork belly from the skillet and set it aside on a plate.
4. Stir-fry Kimchi and Garlic:
    - In the same skillet, add a bit more vegetable oil if needed.
    - Add minced garlic and chopped kimchi to the skillet. Stir-fry for 2-3 minutes until the kimchi is slightly caramelized and fragrant.
5. Add Rice and Pork Belly:
    - Add the cooked rice to the skillet with the stir-fried kimchi and garlic.
    - Stir well to combine all the ingredients.

- Add back the cooked pork belly to the skillet and mix with the rice and kimchi.
6. Make a Well and Add Eggs:
    - Push the rice mixture to one side of the skillet to create a well.
    - Crack the eggs into the well and scramble them until they're cooked through.
7. Combine and Season:
    - Mix the scrambled eggs with the rice mixture until everything is well combined.
    - Season the fried rice with sesame oil, salt, and pepper to taste.
8. Serve Pork Belly Kimchi Fried Rice:
    - Transfer the fried rice to serving plates or bowls.
    - Garnish with chopped green onions and sprinkle with sesame seeds, if desired.
    - Serve hot and enjoy your Pork Belly Kimchi Fried Rice!

This Pork Belly Kimchi Fried Rice is a comforting and flavorful dish that's perfect for any meal. The combination of crispy pork belly, tangy kimchi, and savory rice creates a delicious harmony of flavors. Customize the spice level by adjusting the amount of gochujang or adding crushed red pepper flakes for extra heat. Enjoy this satisfying Korean dish with your favorite side dishes!

Korean BBQ Meatballs

Ingredients:

For the Meatballs:

- 1 pound ground beef or pork
- 1/2 cup breadcrumbs
- 1/4 cup finely chopped onion
- 1 egg
- 2 cloves garlic, minced
- 1 tablespoon soy sauce
- Salt and pepper, to taste
- Vegetable oil, for cooking

For the Korean BBQ Sauce:

- 1/4 cup soy sauce
- 2 tablespoons gochujang (Korean red chili paste)
- 2 tablespoons honey or brown sugar
- 1 tablespoon rice vinegar
- 1 tablespoon sesame oil
- 2 cloves garlic, minced
- 1 teaspoon grated ginger
- 2 green onions, chopped (for garnish)
- Sesame seeds, for garnish

Instructions:

1. Prepare the Meatballs:
    - Preheat the oven to 400°F (200°C).
    - In a mixing bowl, combine ground meat, breadcrumbs, chopped onion, egg, minced garlic, soy sauce, salt, and pepper. Mix until well combined.
    - Shape the mixture into meatballs, about 1 inch in diameter.
2. Cook the Meatballs:
    - Heat a bit of vegetable oil in an oven-safe skillet or frying pan over medium-high heat.
    - Add the meatballs to the skillet and brown them on all sides, about 2-3 minutes per side.
    - Transfer the skillet to the preheated oven and bake for an additional 10-12 minutes, or until the meatballs are cooked through.

3. Make the Korean BBQ Sauce:
    - While the meatballs are baking, prepare the Korean BBQ sauce.
    - In a small saucepan, combine soy sauce, gochujang, honey or brown sugar, rice vinegar, sesame oil, minced garlic, and grated ginger.
    - Bring the sauce to a simmer over medium heat, stirring occasionally. Cook for 2-3 minutes until the sauce thickens slightly.
4. Glaze the Meatballs:
    - Remove the cooked meatballs from the oven.
    - Pour the Korean BBQ sauce over the meatballs, tossing gently to coat them evenly.
5. Serve Korean BBQ Meatballs:
    - Transfer the glazed meatballs to a serving platter.
    - Garnish with chopped green onions and sesame seeds.
6. Enjoy Your Korean BBQ Meatballs:
    - Serve the meatballs hot as an appetizer or main dish.
    - Enjoy the delicious flavors of Korean barbecue in every bite of these savory meatballs!

These Korean BBQ Meatballs make a fantastic appetizer for parties or a flavorful main course served over rice or noodles. Feel free to adjust the spiciness and sweetness of the BBQ sauce according to your taste preferences. This recipe is sure to be a hit with family and friends!

Dak Bulgogi (Korean BBQ Chicken)

Ingredients:

- 1.5 pounds boneless, skinless chicken thighs or breast, thinly sliced
- 4 cloves garlic, minced
- 1/4 cup soy sauce
- 2 tablespoons gochujang (Korean red chili paste)
- 2 tablespoons honey or brown sugar
- 1 tablespoon sesame oil
- 1 tablespoon rice wine or mirin (optional)
- 1 tablespoon grated ginger
- 2 green onions, chopped (for garnish)
- Sesame seeds, for garnish
- Vegetable oil, for cooking

Instructions:

1. Prepare the Marinade:
    - In a bowl, combine minced garlic, soy sauce, gochujang, honey or brown sugar, sesame oil, rice wine or mirin (if using), and grated ginger. Mix well to create the marinade.
2. Marinate the Chicken:
    - Place the thinly sliced chicken in a shallow dish or resealable plastic bag.
    - Pour the marinade over the chicken, making sure all pieces are well-coated.
    - Cover the dish or seal the bag, and marinate in the refrigerator for at least 1 hour, or ideally overnight for maximum flavor.
3. Cook the Chicken:
    - Heat a tablespoon of vegetable oil in a large skillet or grill pan over medium-high heat.
    - Add the marinated chicken to the skillet in a single layer, reserving the marinade.
    - Cook the chicken for 6-8 minutes, stirring occasionally, until it is cooked through and nicely caramelized.
4. Simmer the Sauce (Optional):
    - While the chicken is cooking, pour the reserved marinade into a small saucepan.
    - Bring the marinade to a simmer over medium heat and cook for 3-4 minutes until slightly thickened. This will be used as a sauce for serving.

5. Serve Dak Bulgogi:
    - Transfer the cooked chicken to a serving platter.
    - Drizzle with the simmered marinade sauce (if using).
    - Garnish with chopped green onions and sesame seeds.
6. Enjoy Your Dak Bulgogi:
    - Serve the Dak Bulgogi hot with steamed rice and your favorite Korean side dishes.
    - Enjoy the delicious flavors of this Korean BBQ chicken dish!

Dak Bulgogi is perfect for a quick and flavorful meal that can be enjoyed with family and friends. The marinade adds a wonderful balance of sweet, savory, and spicy flavors to the tender and juicy chicken. Customize the level of spiciness by adjusting the amount of gochujang according to your taste. This dish is sure to be a hit at any dinner table!

Korean BBQ Pork Lettuce Wraps

Ingredients:

For the Pork:

- 1 pound pork shoulder or pork belly, thinly sliced
- 3 tablespoons soy sauce
- 2 tablespoons honey or brown sugar
- 1 tablespoon sesame oil
- 2 cloves garlic, minced
- 1 tablespoon grated ginger
- 1 tablespoon rice wine or mirin (optional)
- Vegetable oil, for cooking

For Serving:

- Fresh lettuce leaves (such as butter lettuce or romaine hearts)
- Ssamjang (Korean dipping sauce)
- Sliced green onions
- Sliced cucumber
- Kimchi
- Cooked rice (optional)
- Sesame seeds, for garnish
- Red chili flakes (gochugaru), for garnish (optional)

Instructions:

1. Marinate the Pork:
    - In a bowl, combine soy sauce, honey or brown sugar, sesame oil, minced garlic, grated ginger, and rice wine or mirin (if using). Mix well to create the marinade.
    - Add the thinly sliced pork to the marinade and toss to coat evenly.
    - Let the pork marinate for at least 30 minutes, or ideally 1-2 hours in the refrigerator.
2. Cook the Pork:
    - Heat a bit of vegetable oil in a large skillet or grill pan over medium-high heat.
    - Add the marinated pork slices to the skillet in a single layer.
    - Cook the pork for 3-4 minutes on each side, or until caramelized and cooked through.

- Remove the cooked pork from the skillet and set aside.
3. Prepare Lettuce Wraps:
    - Wash and dry the lettuce leaves, and arrange them on a serving platter.
    - Place the cooked pork, sliced green onions, sliced cucumber, and kimchi on the platter alongside the lettuce leaves.
4. Assemble and Serve:
    - To assemble the wraps, take a lettuce leaf and place a spoonful of cooked pork inside.
    - Add a dollop of ssamjang (Korean dipping sauce) on top of the pork.
    - Add sliced green onions, cucumber, and kimchi as desired.
    - Optionally, add a spoonful of cooked rice to each wrap for extra substance.
    - Sprinkle sesame seeds and red chili flakes (gochugaru) on top for garnish, if desired.
5. Enjoy Your Korean BBQ Pork Lettuce Wraps:
    - To eat, fold the lettuce leaf around the filling and enjoy the flavorful combination of grilled pork and fresh vegetables.
    - Serve with extra ssamjang and kimchi on the side for dipping and additional flavor.

Korean BBQ Pork Lettuce Wraps are perfect for a light and healthy meal, especially during warmer months. The combination of savory grilled pork, crisp lettuce, and tangy condiments creates a delightful burst of flavors in each bite. Customize the wraps with your favorite vegetables and enjoy the interactive dining experience with family and friends!

Kimchi BBQ Grilled Cheese

Ingredients:

- 4 slices of bread (white, whole wheat, or sourdough)
- 1 cup shredded cheese (cheddar, mozzarella, or a blend)
- 1/2 cup kimchi, drained and chopped
- 2 tablespoons barbecue sauce
- 2 tablespoons butter, softened

Instructions:

1. Prepare the Kimchi BBQ Filling:
    - In a small bowl, mix together the chopped kimchi and barbecue sauce until well combined. Set aside.
2. Assemble the Grilled Cheese Sandwich:
    - Lay out the bread slices on a clean surface.
    - Spread a thin layer of softened butter on one side of each bread slice (this will be the outside of the sandwich when grilled).
    - Flip over two bread slices (buttered side down) and divide the shredded cheese evenly between them, spreading it out to cover the entire surface of the bread.
3. Add the Kimchi BBQ Filling:
    - Spoon the kimchi BBQ mixture over the cheese on each bread slice, spreading it evenly.
4. Assemble and Grill the Sandwich:
    - Place the remaining bread slices on top of the kimchi BBQ filling, buttered side facing up.
    - Heat a non-stick skillet or griddle over medium heat.
    - Carefully transfer the assembled sandwiches to the skillet or griddle.
    - Cook for 3-4 minutes on each side, or until the bread is golden brown and crispy, and the cheese is melted.
    - Press down gently on the sandwiches with a spatula while cooking to help melt the cheese and create an evenly grilled crust.
5. Serve and Enjoy:
    - Once the sandwiches are grilled to perfection, remove them from the skillet.
    - Let them cool for a minute before slicing them in half.
    - Serve hot and enjoy the delicious Kimchi BBQ Grilled Cheese sandwiches!
6. Optional Serving Suggestions:

- Serve the grilled cheese sandwiches with a side of pickles or coleslaw for a complete meal.
- Pair with a bowl of hot soup (such as tomato soup) for a comforting lunch or dinner.
- Enjoy these flavorful sandwiches as a tasty and satisfying snack!

Kimchi BBQ Grilled Cheese sandwiches are a wonderful combination of spicy, tangy, and cheesy flavors. The addition of kimchi and barbecue sauce adds depth and excitement to the classic grilled cheese, making it a must-try for any grilled cheese enthusiast or lover of Korean flavors!

Gochujang BBQ Salmon

Ingredients:

- 4 salmon fillets (about 6 ounces each), skin-on or skinless
- 3 tablespoons gochujang (Korean red chili paste)
- 2 tablespoons soy sauce
- 2 tablespoons honey or brown sugar
- 1 tablespoon sesame oil
- 2 cloves garlic, minced
- 1 tablespoon rice vinegar or apple cider vinegar
- 1 tablespoon grated ginger
- 2 green onions, chopped (for garnish)
- Sesame seeds, for garnish
- Vegetable oil, for cooking

Instructions:

1. Prepare the Gochujang BBQ Marinade:
    - In a bowl, combine gochujang, soy sauce, honey or brown sugar, sesame oil, minced garlic, rice vinegar, and grated ginger. Mix well to create the marinade.
2. Marinate the Salmon:
    - Place the salmon fillets in a shallow dish or resealable plastic bag.
    - Pour the marinade over the salmon, ensuring each fillet is well-coated.
    - Cover the dish or seal the bag, and marinate in the refrigerator for at least 30 minutes, or up to 2 hours for maximum flavor.
3. Cook the Salmon:
    - Preheat the oven to 400°F (200°C).
    - Heat a bit of vegetable oil in an oven-safe skillet or grill pan over medium-high heat.
    - Remove the salmon from the marinade (reserve the marinade for later use) and place the fillets in the skillet, skin-side down if they have skin.
    - Sear the salmon for 2-3 minutes until golden brown on the bottom.
4. Finish Cooking in the Oven:
    - Transfer the skillet with the salmon to the preheated oven.
    - Bake for 8-10 minutes, or until the salmon is cooked to your desired doneness and flakes easily with a fork.
5. Make the Gochujang BBQ Glaze:

- While the salmon is baking, pour the reserved marinade into a small saucepan.
- Bring the marinade to a simmer over medium heat and cook for 3-4 minutes until slightly thickened. This will be used as a glaze for the cooked salmon.

6. Serve Gochujang BBQ Salmon:
    - Remove the cooked salmon from the oven.
    - Brush the salmon fillets with the prepared gochujang BBQ glaze.
    - Garnish with chopped green onions and sesame seeds.
7. Enjoy Your Gochujang BBQ Salmon:
    - Serve the salmon hot with steamed rice and your favorite vegetables.
    - Enjoy the delicious and spicy flavors of this Korean-inspired salmon dish!

Gochujang BBQ Salmon is a fantastic way to enjoy salmon with a unique and bold Korean twist. The marinade adds a perfect balance of sweet, savory, and spicy flavors to the tender and flaky fish. This dish is sure to impress and is great for special occasions or weeknight dinners alike!

Spicy Pork BBQ Nachos

Ingredients:

For the Spicy Pork BBQ:

- 1 pound pork shoulder or pork belly, thinly sliced
- 3 tablespoons gochujang (Korean red chili paste)
- 2 tablespoons soy sauce
- 2 tablespoons honey or brown sugar
- 1 tablespoon sesame oil
- 2 cloves garlic, minced
- 1 tablespoon grated ginger
- 1 tablespoon rice wine or mirin (optional)
- Vegetable oil, for cooking

For Assembling the Nachos:

- Tortilla chips
- Shredded cheese (cheddar, mozzarella, or a blend)
- Sliced jalapeños, for garnish
- Sliced green onions, for garnish
- Sour cream, for serving (optional)
- Kimchi, for serving (optional)

Instructions:

1. Prepare the Spicy Pork BBQ:
    - In a bowl, combine gochujang, soy sauce, honey or brown sugar, sesame oil, minced garlic, grated ginger, and rice wine or mirin (if using). Mix well to create the marinade.
    - Add the thinly sliced pork to the marinade and toss to coat evenly.
    - Let the pork marinate for at least 30 minutes, or ideally 1-2 hours in the refrigerator.
2. Cook the Spicy Pork BBQ:
    - Heat a bit of vegetable oil in a large skillet or grill pan over medium-high heat.
    - Add the marinated pork slices to the skillet in a single layer.
    - Cook the pork for 3-4 minutes on each side, or until caramelized and cooked through.
    - Remove the cooked pork from the skillet and set aside.

3. Assemble the Nachos:
    - Preheat the oven to 375°F (190°C).
    - Arrange a layer of tortilla chips on a large baking sheet or oven-safe platter.
    - Sprinkle shredded cheese over the tortilla chips, covering them evenly.
    - Spread the cooked spicy pork BBQ over the cheese-topped tortilla chips.
4. Bake the Nachos:
    - Place the assembled nachos in the preheated oven.
    - Bake for 8-10 minutes, or until the cheese is melted and bubbly.
5. Add Toppings and Serve:
    - Remove the nachos from the oven.
    - Garnish with sliced jalapeños, green onions, and any other desired toppings.
    - Serve hot with sour cream and kimchi on the side, if desired.
6. Enjoy Your Spicy Pork BBQ Nachos:
    - Serve the nachos immediately while hot and enjoy the delicious combination of spicy pork, melted cheese, and crunchy tortilla chips!

Spicy Pork BBQ Nachos are perfect for a fun and flavorful appetizer or main dish for a party or casual gathering. The spicy Korean BBQ pork adds a unique twist to classic nachos and will surely be a hit with friends and family. Feel free to customize the toppings based on your preferences for a personalized nacho experience!

Grilled Korean BBQ Eggplant

Ingredients:

- 2 medium-sized eggplants
- 2 tablespoons soy sauce
- 2 tablespoons gochujang (Korean red chili paste)
- 1 tablespoon honey or brown sugar
- 1 tablespoon sesame oil
- 2 cloves garlic, minced
- 1 tablespoon rice vinegar
- 1 tablespoon sesame seeds
- 2 green onions, chopped (for garnish)
- Vegetable oil, for brushing

Instructions:

1. Prepare the Eggplant:
    - Wash the eggplants and slice them lengthwise into 1/2-inch thick slices.
    - Place the eggplant slices on a plate or baking sheet.
2. Make the Korean BBQ Marinade:
    - In a bowl, whisk together soy sauce, gochujang, honey or brown sugar, sesame oil, minced garlic, rice vinegar, and sesame seeds. Mix until well combined.
3. Marinate the Eggplant:
    - Brush both sides of the eggplant slices with the Korean BBQ marinade, ensuring they are evenly coated.
    - Allow the eggplant slices to marinate for at least 20-30 minutes to absorb the flavors.
4. Preheat the Grill:
    - Preheat your grill to medium-high heat (around 375-400°F / 190-200°C).
5. Grill the Eggplant:
    - Lightly brush the grill grates with vegetable oil to prevent sticking.
    - Place the marinated eggplant slices on the preheated grill.
    - Grill the eggplant for 3-4 minutes on each side, or until tender and charred with grill marks.
6. Serve Grilled Korean BBQ Eggplant:
    - Remove the grilled eggplant slices from the grill and transfer them to a serving platter.
    - Garnish with chopped green onions.

7. Enjoy Your Grilled Korean BBQ Eggplant:
    - Serve the grilled eggplant slices hot as a side dish or appetizer.
    - Enjoy the smoky flavor of the grilled eggplant combined with the sweet, savory, and spicy Korean BBQ marinade!

Grilled Korean BBQ Eggplant is a wonderful dish that can be served alongside rice or other Korean-inspired dishes. The marinade adds depth and complexity to the eggplant, making it a flavorful and satisfying addition to any meal. This dish is also suitable for vegetarians and vegans, and it's perfect for those looking to enjoy a delicious and healthy grilled vegetable dish with a Korean twist!

BBQ Pork Belly Banh Mi

Ingredients:

For the BBQ Pork Belly:

- 1 pound pork belly, thinly sliced
- 3 tablespoons soy sauce
- 2 tablespoons honey or brown sugar
- 1 tablespoon fish sauce
- 1 tablespoon sesame oil
- 2 cloves garlic, minced
- 1 tablespoon grated ginger
- 1 tablespoon rice vinegar
- 1 tablespoon vegetable oil

For Assembling the Banh Mi:

- French baguettes or sandwich rolls
- Mayonnaise
- Pickled daikon and carrots (Do Chua)
- Fresh cilantro leaves
- Sliced cucumbers
- Sliced jalapeños (optional)
- Sriracha sauce (optional)

Instructions:

1. Marinate and Cook the BBQ Pork Belly:
    - In a bowl, combine soy sauce, honey or brown sugar, fish sauce, sesame oil, minced garlic, grated ginger, and rice vinegar to create the marinade.
    - Add the thinly sliced pork belly to the marinade and toss to coat evenly. Let it marinate for at least 30 minutes, or ideally 1-2 hours in the refrigerator.
    - Heat vegetable oil in a skillet or grill pan over medium-high heat.
    - Add the marinated pork belly slices to the skillet and cook for 3-4 minutes on each side until caramelized and cooked through. Set aside.
2. Prepare the Banh Mi Sandwiches:
    - Slice the French baguettes or sandwich rolls in half lengthwise.
    - Spread a layer of mayonnaise on one side of each baguette.

- Arrange the cooked BBQ pork belly slices on the bottom half of each baguette.
3. Add Toppings:
    - Top the pork belly with pickled daikon and carrots (Do Chua), fresh cilantro leaves, sliced cucumbers, and sliced jalapeños (if using).
4. Finish and Serve:
    - Drizzle Sriracha sauce over the toppings if you like it spicy.
    - Close the sandwiches with the top halves of the baguettes.
    - Serve the BBQ Pork Belly Banh Mi sandwiches immediately and enjoy!

Tips for Serving:

- You can make the pickled daikon and carrots (Do Chua) ahead of time by julienning them and marinating them in a mixture of vinegar, sugar, and salt.
- Customize the sandwich with additional toppings like sliced radishes, lettuce, or pâté for added flavor.
- Serve the Banh Mi sandwiches with a side of Vietnamese-style dipping sauce (Nuoc Cham) for extra flavor.

BBQ Pork Belly Banh Mi sandwiches are a delicious combination of sweet, savory, and tangy flavors, perfect for a satisfying lunch or dinner. Enjoy these flavorful sandwiches with your favorite sides and condiments for a delightful Vietnamese-inspired meal!

Bulgogi Beef Bibimbap

Ingredients:

For the Bulgogi Beef:

- 1 pound beef sirloin or ribeye, thinly sliced
- 1/4 cup soy sauce
- 2 tablespoons brown sugar
- 1 tablespoon sesame oil
- 3 cloves garlic, minced
- 1 tablespoon grated ginger
- 2 green onions, chopped
- 1 tablespoon sesame seeds
- 1 tablespoon vegetable oil, for cooking

For Assembling Bibimbap:

- Cooked white rice
- 4 eggs
- Assorted vegetables (such as spinach, carrots, bean sprouts, zucchini)
- Gochujang (Korean red chili paste)
- Sesame oil, for drizzling
- Sesame seeds, for garnish
- Salt, for seasoning

Instructions:

1. Marinate the Bulgogi Beef:
    - In a bowl, combine soy sauce, brown sugar, sesame oil, minced garlic, grated ginger, chopped green onions, and sesame seeds.
    - Add the thinly sliced beef to the marinade and toss to coat evenly.
    - Let the beef marinate for at least 30 minutes, or ideally 1-2 hours in the refrigerator.
2. Prepare the Vegetables:
    - Cook each type of vegetable separately:
        - Blanch spinach in boiling water for 1-2 minutes, then drain and squeeze out excess water. Season lightly with salt and sesame oil.
        - Julienne carrots and sauté in a pan with a bit of oil until tender-crisp. Season with salt.

- Blanch bean sprouts in boiling water for 3-4 minutes, then drain and season with salt and sesame oil.
- Thinly slice zucchini and sauté in a pan with a bit of oil until tender. Season with salt.

3. Cook the Bulgogi Beef:
   - Heat vegetable oil in a skillet or wok over medium-high heat.
   - Add the marinated beef and cook for 3-4 minutes, stirring frequently, until the beef is cooked through and caramelized. Set aside.
4. Prepare Sunny-Side-Up Eggs:
   - Heat a non-stick skillet over medium heat and add a bit of oil.
   - Crack eggs into the skillet and cook until the whites are set but the yolks are still runny. Remove from heat.
5. Assemble Bibimbap:
   - Divide cooked rice into individual bowls.
   - Arrange cooked bulgogi beef and assorted vegetables on top of the rice.
   - Place a sunny-side-up egg on top of each bowl.
6. Serve with Gochujang Sauce:
   - Serve bibimbap with a side of gochujang (Korean red chili paste) for diners to mix into their bowls according to their spice preference.
   - Drizzle each bowl with a bit of sesame oil and sprinkle with sesame seeds.
7. Mix and Enjoy:
   - To eat, mix everything together thoroughly, including the gochujang sauce, until well combined.
   - Enjoy the delicious flavors and textures of Bulgogi Beef Bibimbap!

Bulgogi Beef Bibimbap is a hearty and satisfying meal that combines tender marinated beef, flavorful vegetables, rice, and a spicy kick from the gochujang sauce. Customize your bibimbap with your favorite vegetables and enjoy this iconic Korean dish with family and friends!

Korean BBQ Pork Stir-fry

Ingredients:

For the Pork Marinade:

- 1 pound pork tenderloin or pork shoulder, thinly sliced
- 3 tablespoons soy sauce
- 2 tablespoons brown sugar or honey
- 1 tablespoon sesame oil
- 2 cloves garlic, minced
- 1 tablespoon grated ginger
- 1 tablespoon rice wine or mirin (optional)
- 1 tablespoon vegetable oil, for cooking

For the Stir-fry:

- 1 tablespoon vegetable oil
- 1 onion, sliced
- 1 red bell pepper, sliced
- 1 green bell pepper, sliced
- 1 cup broccoli florets
- 1 carrot, julienned
- Cooked rice, for serving
- Sesame seeds, for garnish
- Chopped green onions, for garnish

Instructions:

1. Marinate the Pork:
    - In a bowl, combine soy sauce, brown sugar or honey, sesame oil, minced garlic, grated ginger, and rice wine or mirin (if using).
    - Add the thinly sliced pork to the marinade and toss to coat evenly.
    - Let the pork marinate for at least 30 minutes, or up to 2 hours in the refrigerator.
2. Prepare the Vegetables:
    - Heat 1 tablespoon of vegetable oil in a large skillet or wok over medium-high heat.
    - Add sliced onion, red bell pepper, green bell pepper, broccoli florets, and julienned carrot to the skillet.

- Stir-fry the vegetables for 3-4 minutes until they are tender-crisp. Remove the vegetables from the skillet and set aside.

3. Cook the Pork:
    - Heat another tablespoon of vegetable oil in the same skillet over medium-high heat.
    - Add the marinated pork slices to the skillet in a single layer, reserving any leftover marinade.
    - Stir-fry the pork for 3-4 minutes until cooked through and caramelized.
    - Pour in the remaining marinade and cook for an additional minute to create a glaze.
4. Combine and Serve:
    - Return the cooked vegetables to the skillet with the pork.
    - Stir everything together to combine and heat through.
    - Serve the Korean BBQ Pork Stir-fry over cooked rice.
5. Garnish and Enjoy:
    - Garnish the stir-fry with sesame seeds and chopped green onions.
    - Serve hot and enjoy this flavorful Korean BBQ Pork Stir-fry with rice!

Tips:

- Feel free to customize the vegetables based on your preference. You can add mushrooms, snap peas, snow peas, or baby corn to the stir-fry.
- Adjust the sweetness and saltiness of the marinade according to your taste by adding more or less brown sugar and soy sauce.
- Serve the stir-fry with a side of kimchi or pickled vegetables for extra flavor and texture.

This Korean BBQ Pork Stir-fry is a delicious and satisfying dish that's perfect for a quick weeknight meal. The tender and flavorful pork combined with colorful vegetables and savory sauce will surely be a hit at the dinner table!

Spicy Grilled Tofu Skewers

Ingredients:

- 1 block (14-16 oz) extra-firm tofu
- 2 tablespoons soy sauce
- 2 tablespoons gochujang (Korean red chili paste)
- 1 tablespoon honey or maple syrup
- 1 tablespoon sesame oil
- 2 cloves garlic, minced
- 1 tablespoon grated ginger
- 1 tablespoon rice vinegar
- 1 tablespoon vegetable oil, for grilling
- Optional garnishes: sliced green onions, sesame seeds

Instructions:

1. Prepare the Tofu:
    - Start by pressing the tofu to remove excess water. Place the tofu block on a plate lined with paper towels. Place more paper towels on top of the tofu and weigh it down with something heavy (like a cutting board with cans on top). Let it press for about 30 minutes.
    - Once pressed, cut the tofu into cubes, about 1-inch in size.
2. Make the Spicy Marinade:
    - In a bowl, whisk together soy sauce, gochujang, honey or maple syrup, sesame oil, minced garlic, grated ginger, and rice vinegar.
3. Marinate the Tofu:
    - Place the tofu cubes in a shallow dish or resealable plastic bag.
    - Pour the spicy marinade over the tofu, ensuring all pieces are well-coated.
    - Let the tofu marinate for at least 30 minutes to 1 hour, or longer for more flavor. You can marinate it in the refrigerator if desired.
4. Skewer the Tofu:
    - Preheat your grill or grill pan over medium-high heat.
    - Thread the marinated tofu cubes onto skewers, leaving a little space between each piece.
5. Grill the Tofu Skewers:
    - Brush the grill grates with vegetable oil to prevent sticking.
    - Place the tofu skewers on the grill and cook for about 3-4 minutes on each side, or until grill marks appear and the tofu is heated through.
6. Serve and Garnish:

- Remove the grilled tofu skewers from the grill and place them on a serving platter.
- Garnish with sliced green onions and sesame seeds, if desired.

7. Enjoy Your Spicy Grilled Tofu Skewers:
    - Serve the tofu skewers hot as an appetizer or main dish.
    - Enjoy the spicy and savory flavors of the grilled tofu with your favorite side dishes or dipping sauces.

Serving Suggestions:

- Serve the Spicy Grilled Tofu Skewers with a side of steamed rice or noodles.
- Pair them with a fresh salad or stir-fried vegetables for a complete meal.
- Serve with additional gochujang or soy sauce for dipping.

These Spicy Grilled Tofu Skewers are perfect for a vegetarian barbecue or as a flavorful addition to any meal. They are easy to make and packed with delicious Korean-inspired flavors! Adjust the level of spiciness by adding more or less gochujang according to your taste preferences. Enjoy!

Gochujang BBQ Spare Ribs

Ingredients:

- 2 racks of pork spare ribs
- 1 cup gochujang (Korean red chili paste)
- 1/2 cup soy sauce
- 1/4 cup honey or brown sugar
- 2 tablespoons sesame oil
- 4 cloves garlic, minced
- 2 tablespoons grated ginger
- 1 tablespoon rice vinegar
- Salt and pepper, to taste
- Vegetable oil, for grilling

Instructions:

1. Prepare the Spare Ribs:
    - Start by preparing the pork spare ribs. Remove the membrane from the back of the ribs (if present) for better flavor penetration during cooking. Pat the ribs dry with paper towels and season with salt and pepper.
2. Make the Gochujang BBQ Marinade:
    - In a bowl, whisk together gochujang, soy sauce, honey or brown sugar, sesame oil, minced garlic, grated ginger, and rice vinegar until well combined.
3. Marinate the Spare Ribs:
    - Place the prepared spare ribs in a large shallow dish or resealable plastic bag.
    - Pour the Gochujang BBQ marinade over the ribs, ensuring they are well coated.
    - Cover the dish or seal the bag, and refrigerate for at least 4 hours, or ideally overnight, to allow the flavors to develop.
4. Preheat the Grill:
    - Preheat your grill to medium-high heat, around 300-350°F (150-175°C).
5. Grill the Spare Ribs:
    - Remove the marinated spare ribs from the refrigerator and let them come to room temperature while the grill is preheating.
    - Brush the grill grates with vegetable oil to prevent sticking.
    - Place the spare ribs on the grill, bone side down.

- Grill the ribs for about 45 minutes to 1 hour, turning occasionally, until the ribs are cooked through and caramelized. The internal temperature should reach 190-203°F (88-95°C) for tender ribs.
6. Baste with Remaining Marinade:
    - During the last 15 minutes of grilling, brush the ribs with any remaining marinade to create a flavorful glaze.
7. Rest and Serve:
    - Once the ribs are cooked to your liking, remove them from the grill and let them rest for 10 minutes before slicing.
8. Slice and Enjoy:
    - Slice the Gochujang BBQ Spare Ribs between the bones into individual servings.
    - Serve hot and enjoy the delicious and spicy Korean-inspired flavor of these ribs!

Serving Suggestions:

- Serve the Gochujang BBQ Spare Ribs with steamed rice and a side of kimchi or pickled vegetables.
- Garnish with sliced green onions and sesame seeds for added flavor and presentation.
- Enjoy these ribs as a main dish for a barbecue or special dinner occasion.

These Gochujang BBQ Spare Ribs are sure to be a hit with family and friends. The spicy-sweet marinade and tender ribs make this dish irresistible and perfect for lovers of Korean cuisine! Adjust the spice level by adding more or less gochujang according to your preference. Enjoy!

Korean BBQ Beef Sliders

Ingredients:

For the Korean BBQ Beef:

- 1 pound beef (such as ribeye, sirloin, or flank steak), thinly sliced
- 1/4 cup soy sauce
- 2 tablespoons brown sugar
- 2 tablespoons sesame oil
- 3 cloves garlic, minced
- 1 tablespoon grated ginger
- 1 tablespoon rice vinegar
- 1 tablespoon gochujang (Korean red chili paste) - optional for spice
- 1 tablespoon vegetable oil, for cooking

For Assembling the Sliders:

- Slider buns or small dinner rolls
- Gochujang aioli (mix gochujang with mayonnaise)
- Sliced cucumbers
- Pickled daikon and carrots (Do Chua)
- Fresh lettuce or arugula
- Optional: sliced green onions, sesame seeds

Instructions:

1. Prepare the Korean BBQ Beef:
    - In a bowl, whisk together soy sauce, brown sugar, sesame oil, minced garlic, grated ginger, rice vinegar, and gochujang (if using).
    - Add the thinly sliced beef to the marinade and toss to coat evenly.
    - Let the beef marinate for at least 30 minutes, or ideally 1-2 hours in the refrigerator.
2. Cook the Korean BBQ Beef:
    - Heat vegetable oil in a skillet or grill pan over medium-high heat.
    - Add the marinated beef slices to the skillet, reserving any leftover marinade.
    - Cook the beef for 3-4 minutes, stirring frequently, until cooked through and caramelized.
    - Pour in the remaining marinade and cook for an additional 1-2 minutes to create a flavorful sauce. Set aside.

3. Assemble the Sliders:
   - Slice the slider buns or dinner rolls in half horizontally.
   - Spread a layer of gochujang aioli on the bottom half of each bun.
   - Place a few slices of cooked Korean BBQ beef on top of the aioli.
   - Top with sliced cucumbers, pickled daikon and carrots (Do Chua), and fresh lettuce or arugula.
4. Finish and Serve:
   - Place the top half of the slider buns over the assembled sliders.
   - Secure each slider with a toothpick if needed.
   - Optionally, garnish with sliced green onions and sesame seeds on top.
5. Enjoy Your Korean BBQ Beef Sliders:
   - Serve the sliders immediately and enjoy the delicious fusion of flavors!

Serving Suggestions:

- Serve Korean BBQ Beef Sliders as an appetizer, party snack, or main dish.
- Accompany with a side of kimchi or Asian-style coleslaw for extra flavor.
- Customize the sliders with additional toppings such as sliced jalapeños or sriracha for spice lovers.

These Korean BBQ Beef Sliders are perfect for any occasion and will impress your guests with their bold and savory flavors. Enjoy making and sharing these delicious sliders with family and friends!

Spicy BBQ Pork Rice Bowls

Ingredients:

For the Spicy BBQ Pork:

- 1 pound pork shoulder or pork tenderloin, thinly sliced
- 3 tablespoons gochujang (Korean red chili paste)
- 2 tablespoons soy sauce
- 2 tablespoons honey or brown sugar
- 1 tablespoon sesame oil
- 2 cloves garlic, minced
- 1 tablespoon grated ginger
- 1 tablespoon rice vinegar
- 1 tablespoon vegetable oil

For Assembling the Rice Bowls:

- Cooked rice (white rice or brown rice)
- Sliced cucumbers
- Shredded carrots
- Sliced green onions
- Sesame seeds, for garnish
- Optional: kimchi or pickled vegetables for serving

Instructions:

1. Marinate the Spicy BBQ Pork:
    - In a bowl, combine gochujang, soy sauce, honey or brown sugar, sesame oil, minced garlic, grated ginger, and rice vinegar to make the marinade.
    - Add the thinly sliced pork to the marinade and toss to coat evenly.
    - Let the pork marinate for at least 30 minutes, or ideally 1-2 hours in the refrigerator.
2. Cook the Spicy BBQ Pork:
    - Heat vegetable oil in a skillet or wok over medium-high heat.
    - Add the marinated pork slices to the skillet, reserving any leftover marinade.
    - Cook the pork for 4-5 minutes, stirring frequently, until cooked through and caramelized.
    - Pour in the remaining marinade and cook for an additional 1-2 minutes to create a flavorful sauce. Set aside.

3. Assemble the Rice Bowls:
    - Divide cooked rice into serving bowls.
    - Top each bowl of rice with a portion of the spicy BBQ pork.
4. Add Toppings:
    - Arrange sliced cucumbers, shredded carrots, and sliced green onions on top of the BBQ pork.
5. Garnish and Serve:
    - Sprinkle sesame seeds over the rice bowls for garnish.
    - Serve the Spicy BBQ Pork Rice Bowls hot with optional kimchi or pickled vegetables on the side.

Serving Suggestions:

- Customize the rice bowls with additional toppings such as sliced avocado, steamed broccoli, or fried eggs.
- Drizzle extra gochujang sauce or sriracha over the rice bowls for extra spiciness.
- Serve these rice bowls as a complete meal for lunch or dinner.

Enjoy these Spicy BBQ Pork Rice Bowls as a delicious and satisfying dish that's bursting with Korean-inspired flavors! Adjust the level of spiciness by adding more or less gochujang according to your preference. It's a perfect meal to enjoy with family and friends.

Soy Ginger Grilled Steak

Ingredients:

- 1.5 to 2 pounds of steak (such as ribeye, sirloin, or flank steak)
- 1/4 cup soy sauce (use low-sodium if preferred)
- 2 tablespoons honey or brown sugar
- 2 tablespoons sesame oil
- 3 cloves garlic, minced
- 1 tablespoon grated fresh ginger
- 2 tablespoons rice vinegar
- 1 tablespoon vegetable oil (for grilling)
- Salt and pepper, to taste
- Optional garnish: chopped green onions, sesame seeds

Instructions:

1. Prepare the Marinade:
    - In a bowl, whisk together soy sauce, honey or brown sugar, sesame oil, minced garlic, grated ginger, and rice vinegar.
2. Marinate the Steak:
    - Place the steak in a shallow dish or a resealable plastic bag.
    - Pour the marinade over the steak, ensuring it is well coated.
    - Cover the dish or seal the bag, and refrigerate for at least 1 hour, or up to 4 hours for more flavor. Flip the steak halfway through if using a dish.
3. Preheat the Grill:
    - Preheat your grill to medium-high heat.
4. Grill the Steak:
    - Remove the steak from the marinade, allowing excess marinade to drip off.
    - Discard the marinade.
    - Season the steak with salt and pepper on both sides.
    - Lightly oil the grill grates with vegetable oil to prevent sticking.
    - Place the steak on the grill and cook to your desired doneness, flipping halfway through:
        - For medium-rare: Grill for about 4-5 minutes per side.
        - For medium: Grill for about 5-6 minutes per side.
        - Adjust cooking time based on thickness and preferred doneness.
5. Rest and Slice:

- Once cooked to your liking, remove the steak from the grill and let it rest for 5-10 minutes on a cutting board.
- Slice the steak against the grain into thin slices.

6. Serve:
   - Arrange the sliced steak on a serving platter or individual plates.
   - Garnish with chopped green onions and sesame seeds, if desired.
7. Enjoy Your Soy Ginger Grilled Steak:
   - Serve the steak hot with your favorite side dishes, such as steamed rice, grilled vegetables, or a fresh salad.

Serving Suggestions:

- Serve the Soy Ginger Grilled Steak with a side of stir-fried vegetables or a cucumber salad.
- Drizzle any remaining marinade over the sliced steak before serving for extra flavor.
- Enjoy the steak as a main course for a delicious and satisfying meal!

This Soy Ginger Grilled Steak is a wonderful dish that's perfect for a family dinner or special occasion. The marinade adds depth of flavor and ensures the steak is juicy and tender. Try this recipe and impress your loved ones with this tasty grilled steak!

Korean BBQ Chicken Pizza

Ingredients:

For the Pizza Dough:

- 1 pound (16 oz) pizza dough, homemade or store-bought
- Flour, for dusting

For the Korean BBQ Chicken:

- 2 boneless, skinless chicken breasts, thinly sliced
- 1/4 cup soy sauce
- 2 tablespoons honey or brown sugar
- 2 tablespoons gochujang (Korean red chili paste)
- 1 tablespoon sesame oil
- 3 cloves garlic, minced
- 1 tablespoon grated ginger
- 1 tablespoon rice vinegar
- 1 tablespoon vegetable oil, for cooking

For Assembling the Pizza:

- 1 cup shredded mozzarella cheese
- 1/2 cup shredded cooked chicken (from the Korean BBQ chicken)
- 1/4 cup sliced red onion
- 1/4 cup sliced bell peppers (red or green)
- 2 green onions, chopped
- Sesame seeds, for garnish
- Fresh cilantro leaves, for garnish

For Gochujang Drizzle (optional):

- 2 tablespoons gochujang
- 1 tablespoon honey
- 1 tablespoon water

Instructions:

1. Prepare the Korean BBQ Chicken:
    - In a bowl, combine soy sauce, honey or brown sugar, gochujang, sesame oil, minced garlic, grated ginger, and rice vinegar to make the marinade.

- Add the thinly sliced chicken breasts to the marinade and toss to coat evenly.
- Let the chicken marinate for at least 30 minutes, or ideally 1-2 hours in the refrigerator.

2. Cook the Korean BBQ Chicken:
   - Heat vegetable oil in a skillet or grill pan over medium-high heat.
   - Add the marinated chicken slices to the skillet, reserving any leftover marinade.
   - Cook the chicken for 5-6 minutes, stirring frequently, until cooked through and caramelized.
   - Remove the chicken from the skillet and shred it using two forks. Set aside.

3. Preheat the Oven:
   - Preheat your oven to the temperature recommended for your pizza dough.

4. Prepare the Pizza Dough:
   - On a floured surface, roll out the pizza dough into your desired shape and thickness.
   - Transfer the rolled-out dough to a pizza stone or baking sheet lined with parchment paper.

5. Assemble the Pizza:
   - Spread a layer of shredded mozzarella cheese evenly over the pizza dough.
   - Scatter the cooked and shredded Korean BBQ chicken over the cheese.
   - Top with sliced red onion, bell peppers, and chopped green onions.

6. Bake the Pizza:
   - Place the assembled pizza in the preheated oven and bake according to the dough instructions, typically 12-15 minutes or until the crust is golden brown and the cheese is bubbly.

7. Make Gochujang Drizzle (Optional):
   - In a small bowl, whisk together gochujang, honey, and water to make the drizzle sauce.

8. Finish and Serve:
   - Remove the pizza from the oven and let it cool slightly.
   - Drizzle the gochujang sauce over the pizza (if using).
   - Garnish with sesame seeds and fresh cilantro leaves.

9. Slice and Enjoy Your Korean BBQ Chicken Pizza:
   - Slice the pizza into wedges and serve hot.

Serving Suggestions:

- Serve the Korean BBQ Chicken Pizza with additional gochujang drizzle on the side for those who enjoy extra spice.
- Pair the pizza with a crisp salad or pickled vegetables for a complete meal.
- Enjoy this unique and flavorful pizza as a delicious dinner or party appetizer!

This Korean BBQ Chicken Pizza is a delightful combination of savory, sweet, and spicy flavors that will surely impress your family and friends. Customize the toppings based on your preferences and enjoy this fusion pizza creation!

Gochujang BBQ Wings

Ingredients:

For the Gochujang BBQ Sauce:

- 1/4 cup gochujang (Korean red chili paste)
- 3 tablespoons soy sauce
- 3 tablespoons honey or brown sugar
- 2 tablespoons rice vinegar
- 2 cloves garlic, minced
- 1 tablespoon grated ginger
- 1 tablespoon sesame oil
- 1 tablespoon vegetable oil
- Optional: sliced green onions and sesame seeds for garnish

For the Chicken Wings:

- 2 pounds chicken wings, split into drumettes and flats
- Salt and pepper, to taste
- 2 tablespoons vegetable oil (for baking)

Instructions:

1. Preheat the Oven:
    - Preheat your oven to 425°F (220°C) and line a baking sheet with aluminum foil. Place a wire rack on top of the baking sheet.
2. Prepare the Chicken Wings:
    - Pat dry the chicken wings with paper towels to remove excess moisture.
    - Season the chicken wings with salt and pepper to taste.
3. Bake the Chicken Wings:
    - Place the seasoned chicken wings on the wire rack over the prepared baking sheet.
    - Brush the chicken wings with vegetable oil to help them crisp up during baking.
    - Bake in the preheated oven for 35-40 minutes, flipping halfway through, until the wings are golden brown and crispy.
4. Make the Gochujang BBQ Sauce:
    - In a saucepan, combine gochujang, soy sauce, honey or brown sugar, rice vinegar, minced garlic, grated ginger, sesame oil, and vegetable oil.

- Cook over medium heat, stirring constantly, until the sauce is well combined and slightly thickened (about 3-5 minutes).
5. Coat the Chicken Wings with Sauce:
    - Once the chicken wings are cooked and crispy, transfer them to a large bowl.
    - Pour the prepared Gochujang BBQ sauce over the chicken wings and toss to coat evenly.
6. Serve and Garnish:
    - Transfer the Gochujang BBQ wings to a serving platter.
    - Garnish with sliced green onions and sesame seeds, if desired.
7. Enjoy Your Gochujang BBQ Wings:
    - Serve the wings hot and enjoy the spicy, sweet, and savory flavors!

Serving Suggestions:

- Serve the Gochujang BBQ Wings as an appetizer or main dish with steamed rice and vegetables.
- Pair the wings with a refreshing cucumber salad or kimchi for a traditional Korean side dish.
- Adjust the amount of gochujang in the sauce to control the level of spiciness based on your preference.

These Gochujang BBQ Wings are perfect for game day gatherings, parties, or simply as a flavorful treat for yourself. They are easy to make and packed with Korean-inspired flavors that will surely impress your taste buds! Adjust the cooking time to ensure the chicken wings are crispy and cooked through. Enjoy!

Korean BBQ Beef Tacos

Ingredients:

For the Korean BBQ Beef:

- 1 pound beef sirloin or ribeye, thinly sliced
- 1/4 cup soy sauce
- 2 tablespoons brown sugar
- 2 tablespoons sesame oil
- 3 cloves garlic, minced
- 1 tablespoon grated ginger
- 1 tablespoon rice vinegar
- 1 tablespoon gochujang (Korean red chili paste), optional for spice
- 1 tablespoon vegetable oil, for cooking

For Assembling the Tacos:

- Corn or flour tortillas
- Shredded lettuce or cabbage
- Thinly sliced cucumbers
- Kimchi or pickled vegetables
- Sliced green onions
- Sesame seeds, for garnish
- Lime wedges, for serving

Instructions:

1. Prepare the Korean BBQ Beef:
    - In a bowl, whisk together soy sauce, brown sugar, sesame oil, minced garlic, grated ginger, rice vinegar, and gochujang (if using).
    - Add the thinly sliced beef to the marinade and toss to coat evenly.
    - Let the beef marinate for at least 30 minutes, or ideally 1-2 hours in the refrigerator.
2. Cook the Korean BBQ Beef:
    - Heat vegetable oil in a skillet or grill pan over medium-high heat.
    - Add the marinated beef slices to the skillet, reserving any leftover marinade.
    - Cook the beef for 3-4 minutes, stirring frequently, until cooked through and caramelized.

- Pour in the remaining marinade and cook for an additional 1-2 minutes to create a flavorful sauce. Set aside.
3. Assemble the Tacos:
    - Warm the tortillas in a dry skillet or microwave until soft and pliable.
    - Place a spoonful of cooked Korean BBQ beef onto each tortilla.
    - Top with shredded lettuce or cabbage, thinly sliced cucumbers, and kimchi or pickled vegetables.
4. Garnish and Serve:
    - Garnish the Korean BBQ Beef Tacos with sliced green onions, sesame seeds, and a squeeze of fresh lime juice.
5. Enjoy Your Korean BBQ Beef Tacos:
    - Serve the tacos immediately and enjoy the delicious fusion of flavors!

Serving Suggestions:

- Serve the Korean BBQ Beef Tacos with a side of steamed rice or Asian slaw for a complete meal.
- Customize the toppings based on your preference, such as adding sliced avocado or a dollop of sour cream.
- Pair the tacos with a refreshing drink like iced green tea or a Korean-style cocktail.

These Korean BBQ Beef Tacos are a fantastic dish for taco night or any casual gathering. They are easy to make and packed with bold and savory flavors that will surely satisfy your taste buds. Enjoy this fusion of Korean and Mexican cuisines!

Spicy Pork BBQ Lettuce Cups

Ingredients:

For the Spicy Pork BBQ:

- 1 pound pork shoulder or pork tenderloin, thinly sliced
- 3 tablespoons gochujang (Korean red chili paste)
- 2 tablespoons soy sauce
- 2 tablespoons honey or brown sugar
- 1 tablespoon sesame oil
- 3 cloves garlic, minced
- 1 tablespoon grated ginger
- 1 tablespoon rice vinegar
- 1 tablespoon vegetable oil

For Assembling the Lettuce Cups:

- Large lettuce leaves (such as butter lettuce or romaine hearts)
- Thinly sliced cucumber
- Shredded carrots
- Sliced green onions
- Cooked rice or vermicelli noodles (optional)
- Sesame seeds, for garnish
- Lime wedges, for serving

Instructions:

1. Prepare the Spicy Pork BBQ:
    - In a bowl, combine gochujang, soy sauce, honey or brown sugar, sesame oil, minced garlic, grated ginger, rice vinegar, and vegetable oil to make the marinade.
    - Add the thinly sliced pork to the marinade and toss to coat evenly.
    - Let the pork marinate for at least 30 minutes, or ideally 1-2 hours in the refrigerator.
2. Cook the Spicy Pork BBQ:
    - Heat a skillet or wok over medium-high heat.
    - Add the marinated pork slices to the skillet, reserving any leftover marinade.
    - Cook the pork for 5-6 minutes, stirring frequently, until cooked through and caramelized.

- Pour in the remaining marinade and cook for an additional 1-2 minutes to create a flavorful sauce. Set aside.
3. Assemble the Lettuce Cups:
    - Wash and dry the lettuce leaves, then arrange them on a serving platter.
    - Place a spoonful of cooked Spicy Pork BBQ in the center of each lettuce leaf.
4. Add Toppings:
    - Top the Spicy Pork BBQ with thinly sliced cucumber, shredded carrots, sliced green onions, and any other desired toppings.
    - Optionally, add a small amount of cooked rice or vermicelli noodles on top for added texture and substance.
5. Garnish and Serve:
    - Sprinkle sesame seeds over the lettuce cups for garnish.
    - Serve the Spicy Pork BBQ Lettuce Cups with lime wedges on the side for squeezing over the wraps.
6. Enjoy Your Spicy Pork BBQ Lettuce Cups:
    - Roll up the lettuce leaves and enjoy these delicious and flavorful wraps!

Serving Suggestions:

- Serve the Spicy Pork BBQ Lettuce Cups as a light lunch or appetizer.
- Pair them with a side of kimchi or pickled vegetables for a traditional Korean accompaniment.
- Customize the filling with additional toppings such as sliced avocado, chopped peanuts, or cilantro.

These Spicy Pork BBQ Lettuce Cups are a great way to enjoy Korean-inspired flavors in a light and refreshing manner. They make a perfect meal for warm weather or as a healthy alternative to traditional wraps. Enjoy making and savoring these delightful lettuce cups!

Grilled Korean BBQ Cauliflower

Ingredients:

- 1 large head of cauliflower
- 1/4 cup soy sauce (use tamari for gluten-free)
- 2 tablespoons gochujang (Korean red chili paste)
- 2 tablespoons honey or brown sugar
- 2 tablespoons sesame oil
- 3 cloves garlic, minced
- 1 tablespoon grated ginger
- 1 tablespoon rice vinegar
- 2 tablespoons vegetable oil (for grilling)
- Optional garnish: sliced green onions, toasted sesame seeds

Instructions:

1. Prepare the Cauliflower:
    - Remove the leaves and stem from the cauliflower head and cut it into florets. Try to keep them similar in size for even cooking.
2. Make the Korean BBQ Marinade:
    - In a bowl, whisk together soy sauce, gochujang, honey or brown sugar, sesame oil, minced garlic, grated ginger, and rice vinegar until well combined.
3. Marinate the Cauliflower:
    - Place the cauliflower florets in a large bowl or resealable plastic bag.
    - Pour the Korean BBQ marinade over the cauliflower and toss to coat evenly.
    - Let the cauliflower marinate for at least 30 minutes, or ideally 1-2 hours in the refrigerator.
4. Preheat the Grill:
    - Preheat your grill to medium-high heat.
5. Grill the Cauliflower:
    - Brush the grill grates with vegetable oil to prevent sticking.
    - Remove the cauliflower from the marinade, reserving the excess marinade for basting.
    - Place the cauliflower florets on the preheated grill, allowing any excess marinade to drip off.
    - Grill the cauliflower for 10-12 minutes, turning occasionally, until tender and slightly charred. Baste with the reserved marinade during grilling.

6. Serve and Garnish:
    - Transfer the grilled Korean BBQ cauliflower to a serving platter.
    - Garnish with sliced green onions and toasted sesame seeds for extra flavor and presentation.
7. Enjoy Your Grilled Korean BBQ Cauliflower:
    - Serve the cauliflower hot as a delicious side dish or appetizer.

Serving Suggestions:

- Serve the Grilled Korean BBQ Cauliflower alongside steamed rice and other Korean-inspired dishes.
- Use any leftover cauliflower to make flavorful tacos, wraps, or grain bowls.
- Customize the marinade by adjusting the level of spiciness with more or less gochujang according to your taste preferences.

This Grilled Korean BBQ Cauliflower is a wonderful vegetarian dish that's packed with savory, sweet, and spicy flavors. It's perfect for grilling season and a great way to enjoy cauliflower in a new and exciting way. Give this recipe a try and enjoy the delicious results!

Kimchi BBQ Grilled Corn

Ingredients:

- 4 ears of fresh corn, husked
- 1 cup kimchi, chopped
- 1/4 cup Korean barbecue sauce (store-bought or homemade)
- 2 tablespoons sesame oil
- 1 tablespoon soy sauce
- 1 tablespoon honey or brown sugar
- 2 cloves garlic, minced
- 1 tablespoon grated ginger
- Optional garnish: chopped green onions, sesame seeds

Instructions:

1. Prepare the Kimchi BBQ Marinade:
    - In a bowl, combine chopped kimchi, Korean barbecue sauce, sesame oil, soy sauce, honey or brown sugar, minced garlic, and grated ginger. Mix well to combine all the flavors.
2. Marinate the Corn:
    - Place the husked ears of corn in a large dish or shallow pan.
    - Pour the kimchi BBQ marinade over the corn, making sure to coat each ear evenly.
    - Cover and let the corn marinate for at least 30 minutes, or ideally 1-2 hours in the refrigerator.
3. Preheat the Grill:
    - Preheat your grill to medium-high heat.
4. Grill the Corn:
    - Remove the corn from the marinade, reserving the excess marinade for basting.
    - Place the corn on the preheated grill and cook for about 10-12 minutes, turning occasionally, until the corn is tender and charred in spots.
    - While grilling, baste the corn with the reserved marinade to infuse more flavor.
5. Serve and Garnish:
    - Transfer the grilled Kimchi BBQ Corn to a serving platter.
    - Garnish with chopped green onions and sesame seeds for added flavor and presentation.
6. Enjoy Your Kimchi BBQ Grilled Corn:

- Serve the corn hot as a unique and flavorful side dish or appetizer.

Serving Suggestions:

- Serve the Kimchi BBQ Grilled Corn alongside Korean BBQ meats, rice, or other Asian-inspired dishes.
- Enjoy the corn as part of a summer barbecue or outdoor gathering.
- Customize the level of spiciness by adjusting the amount of kimchi or Korean barbecue sauce used in the marinade.

This Kimchi BBQ Grilled Corn is a delightful way to enjoy the bold and tangy flavors of kimchi combined with the smoky sweetness of grilled corn. It's sure to be a hit at your next cookout or meal! Experiment with the marinade ingredients to suit your taste preferences and enjoy this delicious dish.

Spicy Pork BBQ Quesadillas

Ingredients:

For the Spicy Pork BBQ:

- 1 pound pork shoulder or pork tenderloin, thinly sliced
- 3 tablespoons gochujang (Korean red chili paste)
- 2 tablespoons soy sauce
- 2 tablespoons honey or brown sugar
- 1 tablespoon sesame oil
- 3 cloves garlic, minced
- 1 tablespoon grated ginger
- 1 tablespoon rice vinegar
- 1 tablespoon vegetable oil

For the Quesadillas:

- 4 large flour tortillas
- 2 cups shredded cheese (cheddar, Monterey Jack, or Mexican blend)
- 1 cup kimchi, chopped
- 1/4 cup sliced green onions
- Vegetable oil or cooking spray, for cooking

Optional Serving Suggestions:

- Sour cream
- Sliced avocado
- Salsa or pico de gallo

Instructions:

1. Prepare the Spicy Pork BBQ:
    - In a bowl, combine gochujang, soy sauce, honey or brown sugar, sesame oil, minced garlic, grated ginger, rice vinegar, and vegetable oil to make the marinade.
    - Add the thinly sliced pork to the marinade and toss to coat evenly.
    - Let the pork marinate for at least 30 minutes, or ideally 1-2 hours in the refrigerator.
2. Cook the Spicy Pork BBQ:
    - Heat a skillet or wok over medium-high heat.

- Add the marinated pork slices to the skillet, reserving any leftover marinade.
- Cook the pork for 5-6 minutes, stirring frequently, until cooked through and caramelized.
- Pour in the remaining marinade and cook for an additional 1-2 minutes to create a flavorful sauce. Set aside.

3. Assemble the Quesadillas:
    - Heat a large skillet or griddle over medium heat.
    - Place one flour tortilla on the skillet.
    - Sprinkle a layer of shredded cheese over half of the tortilla.
    - Spoon a portion of the cooked Spicy Pork BBQ over the cheese.
    - Top with chopped kimchi and sliced green onions.
    - Fold the empty half of the tortilla over the filling to create a half-moon shape.
4. Cook the Quesadillas:
    - Cook the quesadilla for 2-3 minutes on each side, or until the tortilla is golden brown and crispy, and the cheese is melted.
    - Repeat with the remaining tortillas and filling ingredients.
5. Serve and Enjoy:
    - Cut the cooked quesadillas into wedges.
    - Serve hot with sour cream, sliced avocado, and salsa or pico de gallo on the side.

Serving Suggestions:

- Customize the quesadillas by adding additional toppings such as sliced jalapeños or cilantro.
- Serve the Spicy Pork BBQ Quesadillas as a hearty appetizer, lunch, or dinner option.
- Pair with a fresh salad or Mexican-style rice for a complete meal.

These Spicy Pork BBQ Quesadillas are a flavorful and satisfying dish that combines the best of Korean and Mexican cuisines. The spicy pork, gooey cheese, and tangy kimchi create a delicious flavor profile that will impress your family and friends. Enjoy making and devouring these mouthwatering quesadillas!

Gochujang BBQ Meatloaf

Ingredients:

For the Meatloaf:

- 1.5 pounds ground beef (or a mix of beef and pork)
- 1 cup breadcrumbs
- 1/2 cup milk
- 1 onion, finely chopped
- 2 cloves garlic, minced
- 2 eggs
- 2 tablespoons gochujang (Korean red chili paste)
- 2 tablespoons soy sauce
- 1 tablespoon sesame oil
- 1 tablespoon brown sugar
- Salt and pepper, to taste

For the Gochujang BBQ Glaze:

- 1/4 cup ketchup
- 2 tablespoons gochujang (Korean red chili paste)
- 1 tablespoon soy sauce
- 1 tablespoon brown sugar
- 1 tablespoon rice vinegar

Optional Garnish:

- Thinly sliced green onions
- Toasted sesame seeds

Instructions:

1. Preheat the Oven:
    - Preheat your oven to 375°F (190°C).
2. Prepare the Meatloaf Mixture:
    - In a large mixing bowl, combine the ground beef, breadcrumbs, milk, finely chopped onion, minced garlic, eggs, gochujang, soy sauce, sesame oil, brown sugar, salt, and pepper.
    - Mix well until all ingredients are thoroughly combined.
3. Shape the Meatloaf:
    - Transfer the meatloaf mixture to a baking dish or loaf pan.

- Shape the mixture into a loaf shape, ensuring it is evenly packed.
4. Make the Gochujang BBQ Glaze:
   - In a small bowl, whisk together ketchup, gochujang, soy sauce, brown sugar, and rice vinegar until smooth and well combined.
5. Glaze the Meatloaf:
   - Brush a generous amount of the Gochujang BBQ glaze over the top and sides of the meatloaf, reserving some glaze for basting during cooking.
6. Bake the Meatloaf:
   - Place the meatloaf in the preheated oven.
   - Bake for 50-60 minutes, or until the meatloaf is cooked through and reaches an internal temperature of 160°F (71°C). Baste the meatloaf with the remaining glaze halfway through baking.
7. Rest and Serve:
   - Remove the meatloaf from the oven and let it rest for 10 minutes before slicing.
8. Garnish and Enjoy:
   - Garnish the Gochujang BBQ Meatloaf with thinly sliced green onions and toasted sesame seeds, if desired.
   - Slice and serve the meatloaf warm, and enjoy the flavorful and spicy twist!

Serving Suggestions:

- Serve the Gochujang BBQ Meatloaf with mashed potatoes, steamed rice, or roasted vegetables.
- Use any leftover meatloaf slices for sandwiches or wraps.
- Adjust the level of spiciness by adding more or less gochujang to the meatloaf mixture and glaze.

This Gochujang BBQ Meatloaf is a delightful and savory dish that brings Korean-inspired flavors to a classic comfort food. It's perfect for family dinners and gatherings, offering a unique and delicious take on meatloaf. Enjoy cooking and savoring this flavorful dish!

Korean BBQ Beef Wraps

Ingredients:

For the Beef Marinade:

- 1 pound beef sirloin or ribeye, thinly sliced
- 1/4 cup soy sauce
- 2 tablespoons brown sugar
- 2 tablespoons sesame oil
- 3 cloves garlic, minced
- 1 tablespoon grated ginger
- 1 tablespoon rice vinegar
- 1 tablespoon gochujang (Korean red chili paste) - optional for spice
- 1 tablespoon vegetable oil, for cooking

For Assembling the Wraps:

- Large lettuce leaves (such as butter lettuce or romaine hearts)
- Cooked rice or rice noodles, optional
- Thinly sliced cucumbers
- Shredded carrots
- Sliced green onions
- Kimchi or pickled vegetables
- Sesame seeds, for garnish

Instructions:

1. Prepare the Beef Marinade:
    - In a bowl, whisk together soy sauce, brown sugar, sesame oil, minced garlic, grated ginger, rice vinegar, and gochujang (if using) to make the marinade.
    - Add the thinly sliced beef to the marinade and toss to coat evenly.
    - Let the beef marinate for at least 30 minutes, or ideally 1-2 hours in the refrigerator.
2. Cook the Marinated Beef:
    - Heat vegetable oil in a skillet or wok over medium-high heat.
    - Add the marinated beef slices to the skillet, reserving any leftover marinade.
    - Cook the beef for 3-4 minutes, stirring frequently, until cooked through and caramelized.

- Pour in the remaining marinade and cook for an additional 1-2 minutes to create a flavorful sauce. Set aside.
3. Assemble the Beef Wraps:
    - Wash and dry the lettuce leaves, then arrange them on a serving platter.
    - Place a spoonful of cooked Korean BBQ beef in the center of each lettuce leaf.
    - Add a small portion of cooked rice or rice noodles (if using) on top of the beef.
    - Top with thinly sliced cucumbers, shredded carrots, sliced green onions, and kimchi or pickled vegetables.
4. Garnish and Serve:
    - Sprinkle sesame seeds over the beef wraps for added flavor and presentation.
5. Enjoy Your Korean BBQ Beef Wraps:
    - Roll up the lettuce leaves to enclose the filling and enjoy these flavorful wraps!

Serving Suggestions:

- Serve the Korean BBQ Beef Wraps as a main dish or appetizer.
- Pair with additional side dishes like steamed rice, kimchi, or Korean-style salads.
- Customize the wraps with your favorite toppings and adjust the level of spiciness based on your preference.

These Korean BBQ Beef Wraps are a delightful and interactive meal that's perfect for sharing with family and friends. The combination of savory beef, crisp vegetables, and tangy kimchi wrapped in fresh lettuce leaves creates a delicious and satisfying eating experience. Enjoy making and savoring these flavorful wraps!

Spicy Korean BBQ Potato Salad

Ingredients:

- 2 pounds potatoes (Yukon Gold or red potatoes), peeled and diced into bite-sized pieces
- 1/2 cup mayonnaise
- 2 tablespoons gochujang (Korean red chili paste)
- 2 tablespoons soy sauce
- 1 tablespoon sesame oil
- 2 cloves garlic, minced
- 1 tablespoon rice vinegar
- 1 tablespoon honey or brown sugar
- 1 cup shredded carrots
- 1/2 cup chopped green onions
- Salt and pepper, to taste
- Sesame seeds, for garnish
- Optional: sliced hard-boiled eggs for garnish

Instructions:

1. Boil the Potatoes:
    - Place the diced potatoes in a large pot of salted water.
    - Bring to a boil over medium-high heat and cook for 10-12 minutes, or until the potatoes are fork-tender.
    - Drain the cooked potatoes and let them cool slightly.
2. Prepare the Dressing:
    - In a mixing bowl, whisk together mayonnaise, gochujang, soy sauce, sesame oil, minced garlic, rice vinegar, and honey or brown sugar until smooth and well combined.
3. Assemble the Potato Salad:
    - Place the cooked and slightly cooled potatoes in a large mixing bowl.
    - Add the shredded carrots and chopped green onions to the bowl.
4. Add the Dressing:
    - Pour the prepared dressing over the potatoes and vegetables.
    - Gently toss everything together until the potatoes and vegetables are evenly coated with the dressing.
    - Season with salt and pepper to taste.
5. Chill and Garnish:

- Cover the potato salad and refrigerate for at least 1 hour to allow the flavors to meld together.
- Before serving, garnish with sesame seeds and optionally sliced hard-boiled eggs.

6. Serve and Enjoy:
    - Serve the Spicy Korean BBQ Potato Salad chilled as a side dish or appetizer.
    - Enjoy this flavorful and slightly spicy potato salad alongside grilled meats, sandwiches, or as part of a picnic or potluck spread.

Tips:

- Adjust the amount of gochujang to control the level of spiciness in the potato salad. Add more for a spicier kick or reduce it for a milder flavor.
- You can customize this potato salad by adding other vegetables like diced cucumber, bell peppers, or peas.
- Make sure to taste and adjust the seasoning before serving, as the flavors may develop further after chilling.

This Spicy Korean BBQ Potato Salad is a delightful and unique dish that combines creamy potatoes with bold Korean flavors. It's perfect for adding a spicy twist to your summer gatherings or any meal where you want to impress with a creative and delicious side dish. Enjoy making and savoring this flavorful potato salad!

Soy Garlic BBQ Shrimp

Ingredients:

- 1 pound large shrimp, peeled and deveined
- 3 tablespoons soy sauce
- 3 tablespoons honey
- 2 tablespoons minced garlic
- 2 tablespoons rice vinegar
- 1 tablespoon sesame oil
- 1 tablespoon vegetable oil
- 1 tablespoon finely chopped green onions (scallions), for garnish
- Sesame seeds, for garnish (optional)
- Fresh cilantro, chopped (optional)

Instructions:

1. Prepare the Soy Garlic Marinade:
    - In a bowl, whisk together soy sauce, honey, minced garlic, rice vinegar, sesame oil, and vegetable oil until well combined.
2. Marinate the Shrimp:
    - Place the peeled and deveined shrimp in a large bowl.
    - Pour the soy garlic marinade over the shrimp and toss to coat evenly.
    - Cover the bowl and let the shrimp marinate in the refrigerator for at least 30 minutes, or up to 2 hours for maximum flavor.
3. Preheat the Grill or Skillet:
    - Preheat your grill or a skillet over medium-high heat.
4. Cook the Shrimp:
    - If using a grill, thread the shrimp onto skewers for easier grilling.
    - Place the shrimp skewers or shrimp directly on the grill or in the skillet.
    - Cook the shrimp for 2-3 minutes on each side, or until they turn pink and opaque.
    - Be careful not to overcook the shrimp, as they can become tough and rubbery.
5. Serve and Garnish:
    - Transfer the cooked Soy Garlic BBQ Shrimp to a serving platter.
    - Garnish with finely chopped green onions, sesame seeds, and fresh cilantro, if desired.
6. Enjoy Your Soy Garlic BBQ Shrimp:
    - Serve the shrimp hot as an appetizer or main dish.

- You can also serve the shrimp over rice or alongside steamed vegetables for a complete meal.

Serving Suggestions:

- Serve the Soy Garlic BBQ Shrimp with a side of steamed rice or noodles.
- Pair with a fresh salad or vegetable stir-fry for a balanced and delicious meal.
- Customize the marinade by adjusting the amount of honey or garlic to suit your taste preferences.

This Soy Garlic BBQ Shrimp recipe is quick and easy to make, making it perfect for weeknight dinners or entertaining guests. The savory-sweet flavors of the marinade complement the natural sweetness of the shrimp, creating a mouthwatering dish that everyone will love. Enjoy making and savoring this delightful Soy Garlic BBQ Shrimp!

Korean BBQ Pulled Pork Sandwiches

Ingredients:

For the Pulled Pork:

- 3-4 pounds pork shoulder (pork butt), boneless
- 1 onion, sliced
- 4 cloves garlic, minced
- 1/2 cup soy sauce
- 1/4 cup brown sugar
- 1/4 cup rice vinegar
- 2 tablespoons gochujang (Korean red chili paste)
- 2 tablespoons sesame oil
- 1 tablespoon grated ginger
- 1 cup water
- Salt and pepper, to taste

For the Sandwiches:

- Burger buns or sandwich rolls
- Coleslaw or kimchi (for topping)
- Sliced cucumbers (optional, for crunch)
- Sliced green onions (optional, for garnish)

Instructions:

1. Prepare the Pork Shoulder:
    - Trim excess fat from the pork shoulder and place it in a slow cooker or crockpot.
    - Add sliced onions and minced garlic around the pork.
2. Make the Korean BBQ Sauce:
    - In a bowl, whisk together soy sauce, brown sugar, rice vinegar, gochujang, sesame oil, grated ginger, salt, pepper, and water.
    - Pour the Korean BBQ sauce over the pork shoulder in the slow cooker.
3. Slow Cook the Pork:
    - Cover and cook on low heat for 8-10 hours or on high heat for 4-6 hours, until the pork is very tender and easily pulls apart with a fork.
4. Shred the Pork:
    - Once the pork is cooked and tender, remove it from the slow cooker.
    - Use two forks to shred the pork into bite-sized pieces.

5. Assemble the Sandwiches:
   - Toast the burger buns or sandwich rolls, if desired.
   - Place a generous portion of pulled pork on the bottom half of each bun.
6. Add Toppings:
   - Top the pulled pork with coleslaw or kimchi for a tangy crunch.
   - Optionally, add sliced cucumbers for extra freshness and texture.
7. Garnish and Serve:
   - Sprinkle sliced green onions on top of the pulled pork.
   - Cover with the top half of the bun to complete the sandwiches.
8. Enjoy Your Korean BBQ Pulled Pork Sandwiches:
   - Serve the sandwiches immediately while warm and enjoy the delicious Korean barbecue flavors!

Serving Suggestions:

- Serve Korean BBQ Pulled Pork Sandwiches with a side of pickles, potato salad, or sweet potato fries.
- Add additional gochujang or hot sauce to the pulled pork for extra spice.
- Customize the sandwiches with your favorite toppings and condiments, such as sriracha mayo or sliced jalapeños.

These Korean BBQ Pulled Pork Sandwiches are perfect for a casual meal or party, offering a unique and flavorful twist on classic pulled pork sandwiches. Enjoy making and savoring these delicious sandwiches with family and friends!

Grilled Gochujang Mushrooms

Ingredients:

- 1 pound of your favorite mushrooms (such as cremini, button, or shiitake), cleaned and stems removed if large
- 2 tablespoons gochujang (Korean red chili paste)
- 2 tablespoons soy sauce
- 2 tablespoons honey or brown sugar
- 2 tablespoons sesame oil
- 2 cloves garlic, minced
- 1 tablespoon rice vinegar
- 1 tablespoon vegetable oil, for grilling
- Sesame seeds and sliced green onions, for garnish
- Optional: lime wedges for serving

Instructions:

1. Prepare the Gochujang Marinade:
    - In a bowl, whisk together gochujang, soy sauce, honey or brown sugar, sesame oil, minced garlic, and rice vinegar until well combined.
2. Marinate the Mushrooms:
    - Place the cleaned and stemmed mushrooms in a large bowl.
    - Pour the gochujang marinade over the mushrooms and toss to coat evenly.
    - Let the mushrooms marinate for at least 30 minutes to allow the flavors to absorb.
3. Preheat the Grill or Grill Pan:
    - Preheat your grill or grill pan over medium-high heat.
4. Grill the Mushrooms:
    - Brush the grill grates with vegetable oil to prevent sticking.
    - Thread the mushrooms onto skewers or place them directly on the grill.
    - Grill the mushrooms for 5-7 minutes, turning occasionally, until they are tender and caramelized, and have nice grill marks.
5. Serve and Garnish:
    - Transfer the grilled mushrooms to a serving platter.
    - Sprinkle with sesame seeds and sliced green onions for garnish.
    - Optionally, serve with lime wedges on the side for squeezing over the mushrooms.
6. Enjoy Your Grilled Gochujang Mushrooms:

- Serve the mushrooms hot as a flavorful appetizer or side dish.

Serving Suggestions:

- Serve the Grilled Gochujang Mushrooms alongside steamed rice or as part of a Korean-inspired barbecue spread.
- Use the grilled mushrooms as a filling for tacos, wraps, or sandwiches.
- Add chopped cilantro or Thai basil for a fresh herbaceous flavor.

These Grilled Gochujang Mushrooms are a fantastic way to enjoy the bold and spicy flavors of gochujang with the meaty texture of mushrooms. They make a delicious addition to any meal and are sure to be a hit with mushroom lovers and fans of Korean cuisine alike. Enjoy making and savoring this tasty dish!

Gochujang BBQ Beef Skewers

Ingredients:

- 1.5 pounds beef sirloin or ribeye, cut into 1-inch cubes
- 1/4 cup gochujang (Korean red chili paste)
- 2 tablespoons soy sauce
- 2 tablespoons honey
- 2 tablespoons sesame oil
- 4 cloves garlic, minced
- 1 tablespoon grated ginger
- 1 tablespoon rice vinegar
- 1 tablespoon vegetable oil, for grilling
- Wooden skewers, soaked in water for 30 minutes

Optional Garnish:

- Toasted sesame seeds
- Sliced green onions

Instructions:

1. Prepare the Gochujang BBQ Marinade:
    - In a bowl, combine gochujang, soy sauce, honey, sesame oil, minced garlic, grated ginger, and rice vinegar. Mix well until smooth and well combined.
2. Marinate the Beef:
    - Place the beef cubes in a large bowl or resealable plastic bag.
    - Pour the marinade over the beef and toss to coat evenly.
    - Cover and refrigerate for at least 1 hour, or ideally overnight, to allow the flavors to meld.
3. Assemble the Skewers:
    - Preheat your grill or grill pan over medium-high heat.
    - Thread the marinated beef cubes onto the soaked wooden skewers, leaving a little space between each piece.
4. Grill the Skewers:
    - Brush the grill grates with vegetable oil to prevent sticking.
    - Place the beef skewers on the grill and cook for 8-10 minutes, turning occasionally, until the beef is cooked to your desired doneness and has nice grill marks.

5. Serve and Garnish:
   - Remove the beef skewers from the grill and transfer them to a serving platter.
   - Garnish with toasted sesame seeds and sliced green onions, if desired.
6. Enjoy Your Gochujang BBQ Beef Skewers:
   - Serve the beef skewers hot as a main dish or appetizer.
   - Enjoy them with steamed rice and your favorite Korean side dishes for a complete meal.

Serving Suggestions:

- Serve the Gochujang BBQ Beef Skewers with a side of kimchi, pickled vegetables, or a fresh salad.
- Pair with dipping sauces like gochujang mixed with soy sauce or a Korean-style dipping sauce made with sesame oil, soy sauce, and vinegar.
- Customize the level of spiciness by adjusting the amount of gochujang in the marinade according to your taste preferences.

These Gochujang BBQ Beef Skewers are packed with bold Korean flavors and are perfect for grilling outdoors or indoors on a grill pan. They make a fantastic addition to any barbecue or gathering, offering a delicious taste of Korean cuisine. Enjoy making and savoring these flavorful beef skewers!

Spicy Korean BBQ Brisket Sliders

Ingredients:

For the Spicy Korean BBQ Brisket:

- 2 pounds beef brisket, trimmed of excess fat
- 1 onion, thinly sliced
- 4 cloves garlic, minced
- 1/2 cup soy sauce
- 1/4 cup gochujang (Korean red chili paste)
- 1/4 cup brown sugar
- 2 tablespoons rice vinegar
- 2 tablespoons sesame oil
- 1 tablespoon grated ginger
- 1 cup water
- Salt and pepper, to taste

For Assembling the Sliders:

- Slider buns or mini sandwich rolls
- Spicy Korean BBQ Brisket (from above)
- Kimchi or pickled vegetables
- Sliced cucumber
- Thinly sliced green onions
- Sesame seeds, for garnish

Instructions:

1. Prepare the Spicy Korean BBQ Brisket:
    - Place the beef brisket in a slow cooker or Dutch oven.

- Add sliced onions and minced garlic around the brisket.
- In a bowl, whisk together soy sauce, gochujang, brown sugar, rice vinegar, sesame oil, grated ginger, salt, pepper, and water.
- Pour the sauce over the brisket in the slow cooker or Dutch oven.
- Cover and cook on low heat for 8-10 hours in the slow cooker or at 325°F (165°C) for 3-4 hours in the oven until the brisket is tender and easily shreds.

2. Shred the Brisket:
   - Remove the cooked brisket from the slow cooker or Dutch oven.
   - Use two forks to shred the brisket into bite-sized pieces.

3. Assemble the Sliders:
   - Preheat the broiler in your oven.
   - Split the slider buns or mini sandwich rolls and arrange them on a baking sheet.
   - Place a generous portion of shredded Spicy Korean BBQ Brisket on the bottom half of each bun.

4. Add Toppings:
   - Top the brisket with kimchi or pickled vegetables for a tangy kick.
   - Add sliced cucumber and thinly sliced green onions for freshness.

5. Broil the Sliders:
   - Place the assembled sliders under the broiler for 1-2 minutes, or until the buns are lightly toasted and the toppings are warmed.

6. Garnish and Serve:
   - Sprinkle sesame seeds over the sliders for a final touch.
   - Cover with the top half of the bun to complete the sliders.

7. Enjoy Your Spicy Korean BBQ Brisket Sliders:

- Serve the sliders immediately while warm.
- Enjoy these flavorful sliders as an appetizer or main course!

Serving Suggestions:

- Serve the sliders with additional kimchi, pickled vegetables, or a side salad.
- Pair with sweet potato fries or crispy Asian slaw for a complete meal.
- Customize the sliders with your favorite condiments, such as sriracha mayo or hoisin sauce.

These Spicy Korean BBQ Brisket Sliders are a crowd-pleaser with their bold flavors and tender brisket. They are perfect for parties, game days, or any casual gathering. Enjoy making and savoring these delicious sliders!

BBQ Kimchi Fried Rice Balls

Ingredients:

- 3 cups cooked rice (preferably day-old rice)
- 1 cup chopped kimchi, squeezed of excess liquid
- 1 cup cooked and chopped BBQ pork or chicken (leftover or store-bought)
- 1/2 cup shredded mozzarella cheese (optional)
- 2 green onions, finely chopped
- 2 tablespoons soy sauce
- 1 tablespoon gochujang (Korean red chili paste), optional for spiciness
- 1 tablespoon sesame oil
- 1 tablespoon vegetable oil, for frying
- 1 cup panko breadcrumbs, for coating
- 2 large eggs, beaten
- Salt and pepper, to taste
- Cooking oil spray (optional), for baking

Instructions:

1. Prepare the Fried Rice Mixture:
    - In a large mixing bowl, combine cooked rice, chopped kimchi, cooked BBQ pork or chicken, shredded mozzarella cheese (if using), and chopped green onions.
    - Add soy sauce, gochujang (if using), sesame oil, salt, and pepper. Mix well to combine all ingredients.
2. Form Rice Balls:
    - Take a small handful of the rice mixture and squeeze it firmly into a ball shape using your hands. Repeat until all the rice mixture is used, making approximately 12-15 rice balls.
3. Coat Rice Balls:
    - Prepare two shallow bowls: one with beaten eggs and one with panko breadcrumbs.
    - Dip each rice ball into the beaten eggs, then roll it in the panko breadcrumbs, pressing gently to coat evenly.
4. Fry or Bake the Rice Balls:
    - Option 1 (Frying): Heat vegetable oil in a large skillet over medium heat. Fry the rice balls in batches for 2-3 minutes per side, or until golden and crispy. Transfer to a paper towel-lined plate to drain excess oil.

- Option 2 (Baking): Preheat the oven to 400°F (200°C). Place the coated rice balls on a baking sheet lined with parchment paper. Lightly spray the rice balls with cooking oil spray. Bake for 20-25 minutes, turning halfway through, until golden and crispy.
5. Serve and Enjoy:
    - Serve the BBQ Kimchi Fried Rice Balls hot as an appetizer or snack.
    - Optionally, serve with dipping sauces like soy sauce, gochujang mixed with mayonnaise, or sweet chili sauce.

Serving Suggestions:

- Garnish the rice balls with additional chopped green onions or sesame seeds before serving.
- Enjoy the rice balls on their own or alongside a fresh salad or steamed vegetables for a complete meal.
- Make a larger batch and serve them at parties or gatherings as a unique and tasty finger food.

These BBQ Kimchi Fried Rice Balls are crispy on the outside, savory and flavorful on the inside, and perfect for anyone who loves Korean-inspired dishes. They make a great appetizer or snack for any occasion. Enjoy making and savoring these delicious rice balls!

www.ingramcontent.com/pod-product-compliance
Lightning Source LLC
LaVergne TN
LVHW081558060526
838201LV00054B/1954